Great Tours!

AMERICAN ASSOCIATION FOR STATE AND LOCAL HISTORY BOOK SERIES

ABOUT THE SERIES

The American Association for State and Local History Book Series publishes technical and professional information for those who practice and support history, and addresses issues critical to the field of state and local history. To submit a proposal or manuscript to the series, please request proposal guidelines from AASLH headquarters: AASLH Book Series, 1717 Church St., Nashville, Tennessee 37203. Telephone: (615) 320-3203. Fax: (615) 327-9013. Web site: www.aaslh.org.

ABOUT THE ORGANIZATION

The American Association for State and Local History (AASLH) is a nonprofit educational organization dedicated to advancing knowledge, understanding, and appreciation of local history in the United States and Canada. In addition to sponsorship of this book series, the Association publishes the periodical *History News*, a newsletter, technical leaflets and reports, and other materials; confers prizes and awards in recognition of outstanding achievement in the field; and supports a broad education program and other activities designed to help members work more effectively. To join the organization, contact: Membership Director, AASLH, 1717 Church St., Nashville, Tennessee 37203.

Great Tours!

Thematic Tours and Guide Training for Historic Sites

Barbara Abramoff Levy
Sandra Mackenzie Lloyd
Susan Porter Schreiber

A Division of
ROWMAN & LITTLEFIELD PUBLISHERS, INC.
Lanham • New York • Toronto • Oxford

AltaMira Press
A division of Rowman & Littlefield Publishers, Inc.
4501 Forbes Boulevard, Suite 200
Lanham, MD 20706

PO Box 317
Oxford
OX2 9RU, UK

British Library Cataloguing-in-Publication Information Available

Library of Congress Cataloging-in-Publication Data

Levy, Barbara Abramoff, 1949–
Great tours! : thematic tours and guide training for historic sites / Barbara Abramoff Levy, Sandra Mackenzie Lloyd, Susan Porter Schreiber.
p. cm.—(American Association for State and Local History book series)
Includes bibliographical references and index.
ISBN 0-7591-0098-5 (cloth : alk. paper)—ISBN 0-7591-0099-3 (pbk. : alk. paper)
1. Historic sites—Interpretive programs—United States—Planning. 2. Tour guides (Persons)—Training of—United States. 3. United States—History, Local—Study and teaching—Handbooks, manuals, etc. 4. Curriculum planning—United States—Handbooks, manuals, etc. 5. Personnel management—United States—Handbooks, manuals, etc. I. Lloyd, Sandra Mackenzie, 1953– II. Schreiber, Susan Porter, 1947– III. Title. IV. Series.

E159 .L488 2001
917.304'068'3—dc21 2001034313

Printed in the United States of America

™ The paper used in this publication meets the minimum requirements of American National Standard for Information Sciences—Permanence of Paper for Printed Library Materials, ANSI/NISO Z39.48–1992.

Contents

Foreword vii

Acknowledgments ix

Preface xi

PART ONE: DEVELOPING THE THEMATIC TOUR

Introduction 3

1 *Preparation:* **Assemble the Facts** 7

2 *Planning:* **The Theme Development Team and the Roundtable Workshop** 11

Activity 2.1: Summarizing the Site's Significance on an Index Card—The Storyline 22
Reading 2.1: Storylines, Themes, Physical Evidence, Biographies, and Historical Context 23
Activity 2.2: Material Culture and Biography in a Historic House Setting 26
Roundtable Worksheet 2.1: Using Material Culture and Biography to Interpret Historic Sites 27
Roundtable Worksheet 2.2: Using Material Culture and Biography to Build an Interpretive Tour 28
Activity 2.3: Identifying the Site's Topics 29
Activity 2.4: Identifying the Site's Themes 31
Roundtable Worksheet 2.3: Outline: Using Sentences, Historical Context, Biographies, and Physical Evidence to Build Themes 34

3 *Creating:* **Writing, Revising, and Testing the Thematic Tour Outline** 37

Site Staff Activity 3.1: Revising the Storyline for the Site 40
Site Staff Activity 3.2: Building the Thematic Tour Outline 41
Reading 3.1: Storylines, Themes, Physical Evidence, Biographies, and Historical Context: Pulling It All Together 43
Site Staff Worksheet 3.1: Drafting a Tour Outline 44
Site Staff Activity 3.3: Testing the Thematic Tour Outline 45
Site Staff Activity 3.4: Refining the Thematic Tour Outline 47
Site Staff Activity 3.5: Testing and Revising the Thematic Tour Outline 49

Sample Materials 51

Sample Material 3.1: Time Line for the Caleb Crawley House, 1763–81 52
Sample Material 3.2: Short Biographies for the Caleb Crawley House 54

PART TWO: TRAINING GUIDES TO GIVE THEMATIC TOURS

Introduction 59

4 *Site Specifics and Historical Context* 61

5 *Material Culture:* **The Physical Evidence** 67

Activity 5.1: Understanding Material Culture 69
Reading 5.1: Interpreting Material Culture: A Five-Step Approach 71
Reading 5.2: Asking Questions of Material Culture 73

Activity 5.2: How to "Read" an Artifact 77
Worksheet 5.1: Five Steps to Interpret Material Culture 78
Activity 5.3: Material Culture in a Historic House Setting 79
Worksheet 5.2: Using Material Culture to Build an Interpretive Tour 80

6 *Interpretive Themes and the Thematic Tour* **81**

Activity 6.1: Thematic Tours vs. Non-thematic Tours 86
Activity 6.2: An Introduction to the Components of a Thematic Tour—Storylines, Themes, Physical Evidence, Biographies, and Historical Context 87
Activity 6.3: The Storyline 88
Activity 6.4: Historical Context—*Discussion* 89
Activity 6.5: Finding the Site's Topics 90
Activity 6.6: Identifying the Site's Themes 91
Activity 6.7: Historical Biographies: Interpreting Multiple Perspectives, Part 1 92
Worksheet 6.1: Interpreting Multiple Perspectives: People, Places, Objects, and Themes 94
Activity 6.8: Interpreting Multiple Perspectives, Part 2 95
Activity 6.9: Using the Evidence to Communicate Themes 96
Worksheet 6.2: Using Evidence to Interpret Themes 97
Activity 6.10: Practice, Practice, Practice 98

7 *Communication:* Audience and Presentation Techniques **101**

Activity 7.1: Field Assignment—Taking a Tour 103
Worksheet 7.1: Taking a Tour from the Audience Perspective 105
Activity 7.2: A Communication Model 106
Reading 7.1: Good Communication Skills: *Tips for Guides* 108
Activity 7.3: Adapting the Message to the Audience 109
Activity 7.4: Working with People of Different Ages—Children, Adolescents, and Adults 111
Reading 7.2: The Five Stages of Human Learning: *Tips for Guides* 112
Activity 7.5: Special Needs Audiences 113
Activity 7.6: Interpreting Sensitive Topics to the Public, Part 1 114
Reading 7.3: Interpreting Slavery at Historic Sites: *Tips for Guides* 116
Activity 7.7: Interpreting Sensitive Topics to the Public, Part 2 117
Activity 7.8: Voice 118
Activity 7.9: Gesture 122

PART THREE: MANAGING GUIDES EFFECTIVELY

8 *Managing Guides Effectively* **127**

Form 8.1: Duties of the Guiding Staff at the Caleb Crawley House 129
Form 8.2: Caleb Crawley House Interpretive Guide Application 132
Form 8.3: Caleb Crawley House Guide Agreement 134
Form 8.4: Guide Training Checklist 136
Form 8.5: Mentor/Trainee Agreement 137
Form 8.6: Mentor Checklist 138
Form 8.7: Caleb Crawley House Program Review 142
Form 8.8: Caleb Crawley House Annual Tour Review 144
Form 8.9: Self-Evaluation Questionnaire 148

Bibliography **149**

About the Authors **155**

Index **157**

Foreword

THE PRIMARY GOAL OF *GREAT TOURS!* IS TO PROVIDE A PRACTICAL and easy-to-use tool to help historic sites improve their tours and invigorate guide training. As is often the case, creating an "easy-to-use" book proved to be easier said than done. *Great Tours!* followed a complicated path that involved many people, lots of sites, and more than a decade of development, writing, testing, and refining.

Its genesis occurred in 1989 when Susan Schreiber, as Director of Interpretation and Education for the National Trust for Historic Preservation, organized the first of several retreats in Washington, D.C., for staff working at National Trust sites all over the country. The retreats focused on activities that aimed to identify those qualities and stories that made each site meaningful to the general public. They also explored strategies and methods that could help bring historic resources to life for visitors. National Trust staff left these retreats with certain skills and evident enthusiasm that would help them to begin improving the quality of their site's tours. Still, subsequent conversations made it clear that the site staff needed more than annual retreats to fulfill this ambition.

At first, it seemed that the solution was to write a good guide training curriculum. Renee Friedman, who developed a landmark program for creating thematic tours at Historic Hudson Valley in New York, began work on the curriculum by doing core research and writing. Renee moved on to other work, but Susan and her colleagues at the National Trust remained constant in their vision of a guide training manual for National Trust sites. In 1996, she enlisted Barbara Levy and Sandy Lloyd, both of whom had been involved with the retreats, to explore ways to continue the project. As a first step, we designed and ran a two-day pilot workshop for educators, curators, directors, and guides at all National Trust sites. Using the Woodrow Wilson House in Washington, D.C., as a case study, the workshop included hands-on sessions that addressed tour content, how to work with themes, analysis of material culture, development of thematic tours, how to understand audiences, presentation techniques, and staff management. For two days, we explored many of the issues discussed in this book and led a "test run" for many of its activities. In tandem with the workshop, we drew on the original curriculum and developed a guide training manual. This manual provided participants with the tools they needed to create effective guide training programs at their sites.

The results of the workshop and the feedback on the manual were encouraging. But a problem remained. A good guide training program had to be built on a *great* tour. We found that a *great* tour needed key ingredients: a strong, well-organized outline that stressed excellent research; the development of central themes; the use of pertinent historical context; and the presentation of engaging "people stories" that helped connect contemporary audiences with the past. We wanted to find ways to help sites progress from good tours to *great tours* and, once those great tours were in place, use a guide training program that would encourage the best results from the people who work with the public.

When we decided to turn our guide training manual into a full-fledged book, we knew we had to rethink the way the material was organized. This took months. Our revelation occurred when it became clear that we needed to write part 1, Developing the Thematic Tour (chapters 1–3). This section is designed for site staff and offers a process for creating an outline for a great thematic tour *before* beginning guide training. Part 2, Training Guides to Give Thematic Tours (chapters 4–7), a much revised version of the original guide training manual, is designed to give guides the skills they need to do a great job. Part 3, Managing Guides Effectively (chapter 8) establishes the management framework needed to ensure a supportive and professional environment for guides.

The admittedly circuitous route of this book's development was blessed by the joy of collaboration. In *Great Tours!* the collaboration was intense, and both the concept and writing evolved organically. Each member of our team brought different strengths and skills to the table and each person drafted specific chapters. Barbara, who has many years of experience in interpretation planning and implementation, developed the conceptual framework that informs much of *Great Tours!* She wrote the first drafts of the chapters related to themes, thematic tours, and presentation. Sandy, with extensive background in history and material culture interpretation, drafted the chapters related to tour content, material culture, and audience. Susan, whose work with the historic sites of the National Trust gave her an unusual perspective on the process of change, contributed the section on managing guides. Susan provided the inspiration and the forum in which the book was developed; Barbara and Sandy did the lion's share of writing; and Sandy, our "channeller," provided the voice for the whole.

As the book evolved, so did our partnership. By the time *Great Tours!* was ready for publication, it was difficult for us to draw clear lines showing who did what. Like a jazz trio, we took off on each other's ideas, improvising and embellishing as we solved problems. We challenged each other's assumptions and rewrote each other's work. We tested ideas in the field and then shared our results, all the while molding and shaping the text, the activities, and the overall organization. We worked together to come to reasoned conclusions based on our knowledge and experience, and then we put the ideas into practice in the field. For us, the whole is greater than the sum of the parts. This book was truly a collaboration in spirit and substance, as is the process of developing great tours and training great guides.

Acknowledgments

MANY PEOPLE HAVE HELPED SHAPE THIS BOOK OVER THE course of a decade. Frank E. Sanchis, Vice President, Stewardship of Historic Sites, at the National Trust for Historic Preservation from 1986 to 1999, wanted visitors to leave each site excited by what they had learned and committed to the goals of historic preservation. He recognized that great architecture and carefully preserved collections were not enough and that the quality of the visitor's experience depended more often than not on the quality of the guided tour that was the core interpretive program. As an architect and a can-do preservationist, he wanted to believe that the task of developing great tours could be accomplished simply and with dispatch. The reality proved different, and the process of developing an approach to interpretive planning and guide training evolved over a decade. Frank's support never flagged, nor did his expectations. He sought funding from The L. J. Skaggs and Mary C. Skaggs Foundation, which generously provided initial project support, as well as multiyear support for interpretation at National Trust sites, including support for numerous training programs and interpretive planning activities that contributed to this book. Larry Goldschmidt, Administrative Director and keeper of the National Trust historic sites department budget, was always resourceful in finding funds for workshops, travel, and consultants. An anonymous donor provided funding to complete the manuscript. Richard Moe, President of the National Trust, was unwavering in his support for excellent interpretation at National Trust sites and for this book. Current Vice President James Vaughan provided advice and help with final arrangements.

A number of leaders in historic site interpretation made presentations at National Trust workshops. Their contributions made their way into program development at National Trust sites, and ultimately into this book. In particular, Renee Friedman's approach to thematic interpretation encouraged many sites to see their stories in new ways. Renee, former Director of Museum Programs at Historic Hudson Valley, taught us to outline the steps needed to develop thematic messages, and her early draft of the guide training manual began the process of testing thematic interpretation at historic sites. Barbara Carson, Associate Professor/Adjunct at George Washington University and the College of William and Mary, contributed a methodology for exploring material culture based on work she had done with her husband, Cary Carson, Vice President of Research at Colonial Williamsburg. Their strategy for using an artifact to evoke the lives of the many people who came in contact with it over time informs much of chapter 5, Material Culture: *The Physical Evidence*. We are indebted to Peter Gittleman, Director of Interpretation and Education at the Society for the Preservation of New England Antiquities, whose clear-headed thinking about thematic interpretation, guide training, and tour development significantly influenced us. Many of the activities related to thematic interpretation evolved from Peter's early work in the field. Special thanks go to Margaret Piatt, formerly the Associate Director of Education and Public Programs at Old Sturbridge Village and a veteran interpreter, educator, and producer of historic theater. Margaret conducted workshops for the National Trust on voice control, body language, and presentation techniques. Her work informs many of the activities found in chapter 7, Communication: *Audience and Presentation Techniques*.

Staff from several National Trust sites and other museum professionals served as an advisory committee in the early stages of the book. They include Judy Beil (Lyndhurst), Candace Boyer (Montpelier), Valerie Coons (Old Sturbridge Village), Michelle Craig (Decatur House), Pat Kahle (Shadows-on-the-Teche), Meggett Lavin (Drayton Hall), Cindy Mooney (Lyndhurst), and Peggy Whitworth (Brucemore). In particular, Judy Beil and Cindy Mooney used an early version of the guide training manual to design a new tour for Lyndhurst. They gave us valuable information about what worked and what did not. Jennifer Esler, formerly the Director at Cliveden, a National Trust site in Philadelphia, also supported the initiative. Marsha Gregory was the able project assistant who kept the committee organized. Ann Grogg, while editing an early version of the manual, helped focus the organization of the material.

A number of sites responded to a query for sample evaluation forms and other tools needed to hire and keep good guides. Special thanks go to Peter Gittleman and especially Meggett Lavin, former Curator of Education and Research at Drayton Hall, without whom part 3, Managing Guides Effectively, could not have been written. Meggett created a wonderful environment for guides at Drayton Hall, finding concrete ways to support and encourage guides to do a great job. Thanks also go to Lauri Lechner of Drayton Hall, who supplied revised and updated forms. Materials that address the complex issues inherent in topics that are sensitive both historically and for contemporary audiences draw on the experience of those National Trust sites that interpret slavery. In particular, Beth Taylor of Montpelier contributed the helpful tip sheet, "Interpreting Slavery at Historic Sites—Tips for Guides."

We tested many of the ideas and activities found in this book at sites, conferences, and workshops all over the country. We are grateful to many historic sites and organizations who provided opportunities to test aspects of our ideas, including: Albuquerque Museum of Art and History; American Association for State and Local History (AASLH); Bay State Historical League (BSHL); Betsy Ross House; Belle Grove; Chesterwood; Cliveden; Concord Museum; Conner Prairie; Decatur House; Fairmount Park Houses of the Philadelphia Museum of Art; Filoli; Glessner House Museum; The Highlands; Historic Morven; Illinois & Michigan Canal Corridor Association; Kalamazoo Valley Museum; Louisiana State Museum; Lyndhurst; the McFaddin-Ward House; Molly Brown House Museum; Montpelier; the National Park Service (NPS); the National Trust for Historic Preservation; Oatlands; Pennsbury Manor; Pocumtuck Valley Memorial Association; Shell River Road Museum; the Society for the Preservation of New England Antiquities (SPNEA); the University of Massachusetts; Washington's Crossing; Woodlawn; and Woodrow Wilson House.

We are grateful for the advice, encouragement, and patience of the staff of AltaMira Press, particularly Mitch Allen and Pam Winding, who provided initial assistance, and Susan Walters, our able editor. Susan's enthusiasm, support, clear thinking, and excellent advice have been critical. Her gentle humor made working with her a pleasure. We are likewise grateful for the help, encouragement, and patience of our production editor, John Calderone. Terry Davis, Director of AASLH, also helped pave the way for this collaborative venture between AltaMira and the National Trust.

These acknowledgments would not be complete without mentioning the work of Sam H. Ham, particularly his book *Environmental Interpretation: A Practical Guide for People with Big Ideas and Small Budgets*. We were, and continue to be, inspired by his practical, straightforward, "can-do" approach to the interpretation of natural resources and the environment.

Thanks to our families and friends. You were there through thick and thin and even took some tours with us.

Great Tours! has been an incredible journey, made better by the help we have had from so many people. Thank you for making our work better. Any mistakes are ours.

Preface

Welcome to the Caleb Crawley House! I'm really glad you found the entrance. We just took down the sign yesterday to have it painted. My name is Mrs. Dodge and I will be your guide today. I am sure you have all heard of Caleb Crawley. He was the first person to . . . oops . . . before we get to that I almost forgot, we charge an admission fee of $3.00 per person, so if you will step over here let's take care of that. Before I do that, though, let me ask you not to take any photographs inside the house and, if you would, leave your umbrellas here. It's not raining too hard and we wouldn't want them to drip inside Mr. Crawley's beautiful house would we?

Now, where was I? Oh dear, I can't quite remember, so let's just head toward the house and you can see Mr. Crawley's garden as we go. It's a little early in the season so there is not much in bloom, but just use your imagination because in June there are lots of roses. Please step this way and watch out for the puddles.

Ah, here we are. Isn't Mr. Crawley's front door just lovely? Makes you realize we don't make 'em like we used to. Now I just need to find the key so we can go in. I know it's in here somewhere. Gosh, there it is buried in some tissues. Okey dokey, now let's go inside.

Isn't this front hall just something else? Those dentil cornices and Palladian windows are considered by many to be second only to those at Mount Vernon. Mr. Crawley had the most exquisite taste, which you can see in the superb Chippendale chairs, which are similar to what we think he most likely would have had because his taste was so exquisite. If you step this way you will see another fine example of the type of furniture which we feel sure Mr. Crawley would have owned—this absolutely fabulous escritoire that we just had appraised and is the most valuable thing in the house. The curator won't tell us how much it's worth. She just said to make sure nobody got near it. But, isn't it just lovely? Now if you don't have any questions, please follow me into the parlor, which is where Mr. Crawley played loo with George Washington.

Loo? Where is the loo? I'm sorry. We have no rest rooms in the house. Mr. Crawley of course used a privy, which you may remember seeing as we walked through the garden. We have some modern facilities back at the visitors' center, so if you can wait an hour you can use them then.

Now where was I?

Guided tours are often the primary way people learn about historic sites. The best guided tours breathe life into houses, landscapes, objects, events, and people of the past. They cause us to reflect as we listen, and make us curious to learn more when we leave. They stimulate questions, stir conversation, and cause us to compare historic lives with our own. Good tours may prompt us to take a photograph that, for years, will trigger pleasant memories about an event in our own lives. They may remind us, too, of something we learned about the past, whether it is the bloodshed on a battlefield or the smoke that poured from an old coal stove.

A bad tour tends to do just the opposite. As with the exaggerated Caleb Crawley House example, it can become an experience that feels like it has no beginning, no middle, and seemingly, no end. Such tours are often led by a well-meaning guide who loves the site but recites random facts, offers peripheral comments, and uses words we may not know. The guide's enthusiasm and dedication are obvious, so we shuffle obediently through rooms, listening and looking. As we leave, we politely thank the guide for the tour. We head for the car, promptly hit the gas, and forget anything we might have heard. Or worse, we may remember the tour as a thoroughly bad experience, memorable solely because we had trouble finding the entrance or we had a guide who droned on endlessly.

A mediocre tour, on the other hand, can be a pleasant enough experience. We may walk to our car and think, "what a pretty house." Or we might drive out with a random mix of thoughts about what we heard, and did not hear, during our tour:

What *is* a loo?
What *did* Caleb Crawley do?
Hmm, wish we could have spent more time in the garden.
Gee, I wish I had spent more time looking for a birthday present for Aunt Louise in the gift shop.

As we head out, these thoughts dissolve and memories of our very recent tour fade. If asked later about our visit we might offer a positive, but vague comment: "oh yes, that is a pretty house." If pressed for more information or a good reason to visit, we may well be unable to recall any interesting *ideas* we learned at this historic site. So, while not truly bad, a mediocre tour still fails, as it does not provide our visitors with the richest and best experience that each site has the *potential* to offer.

No site *intends* to give a bad tour, or even a mediocre tour. Sometimes they just happen. But the fact is, too few guides focus—*really* focus—on precisely the experience they want the public to have.

To ensure a vibrant future, historic sites must pay attention to the guided tours they give the public. Visiting historic sites is a leisure time activity. Some people *choose* to tour a site because they are interested in the past or are curious about a particular place. Others choose to take a tour because they have out-of-town visitors or are enjoying an outing with family. These visitors are interested in an educational experience, but it must be one that is engaging rather than heavy, entertaining but informative. Historic sites cannot assume that people will be fascinated to hear every detail about the past, nor that they have hours to spend. Certainly, historic sites must present interpretations that have historical integrity. However, they also must honor the needs of modern audiences whose time, interest, and attention can be limited. Rather than view this as a problem, sites can accept this reality and concentrate on presenting the *most* important information to the public.

One way of thinking about the focus of a guided tour is to consider the question,

What does our site illustrate best about the past?

In thinking about this question, a site can begin to identify its "messages," the important ideas that visitors should hear and then carry home with them.

Next, a site must consider how its resources—its buildings, landscape, collections of objects and documents, programs, and staff—can be used to illustrate its historical messages. These resources, and their authenticity, make a visit to a historic site different from reading a book about the past or visiting a theme park that reconstructs a fantasy past. So the next question a site should ask is,

How can we use our resources to amplify and communicate our site's historical messages?

The final questions build on the first two,

How can we link our messages and our resources to develop a great tour for visitors?

How can we present great history and connect with contemporary lives and interests?

This book describes a series of steps designed to achieve improved interpretation, the essential foundation for creating informative, memorable guided tours at historic sites. Well-researched and well-organized history, illustrated and amplified by a site's unique collections, can powerfully convey a site's messages and overall significance to a broad public. This can happen through a variety of media, including exhibits, publications, videos, programs, and hands-on demonstrations. But, given their prevalence at historic sites, it must occur in guided tours as well. For, when a skilled guide connects well with visitors, there is that certain energizing spark of *people interacting with people* that ignites and encourages the learning process.

To promote the *possibility* of this positive experience, historic sites must train their guides with care, direction, and enthusiasm. To promote the *likelihood* of this experience, this book recommends that sites develop a specific type of tour, a **thematic tour**. A thematic tour serves both the site and the visitor because it organizes the important information that makes the site distinctive in ways that help visitors learn and remember. Because this concept is crucial, **part 1 outlines a strategy to help sites develop and implement thematic tours.** The site should start by developing a thematic tour that will be its core tour: one that it will give regularly to the general public. Later, it can create tours using other important and interesting themes. Part 1 is directed to site staff and others associated with the site who will work to develop this core thematic tour. Developing this tour will help sites take full advantage of the guide training activities described in part 2.

Part 2 offers site staff a strategy to train guides to give thematic tours. Chapters 4–7 are organized by topic: *Site Specifics and Historical Context, Material Culture, Interpretive Themes and the Thematic Tour,* and *Communication.* Each chapter has a selection of related training activities to help guides master the necessary components of a thematic tour as well as the techniques required to give such a tour. The activities are generally arranged in a sequence that moves from relatively easy to more difficult. Trainers should familiarize themselves with all of the activities then choose a menu that suits the particular circumstances of the site and guide staff. A good guide must be creative and flexible. A good guide trainer will use this book in just the same way. By reading through the chapters and their activities, then planning carefully, a trainer can tailor a training program to the site and the people connected with it. **Part 3** (chapter 8, *Managing Guides Effectively*) **includes sample job descriptions, tools for evaluation of guide performance, and strategies for supporting and monitoring the guide staff**.

Central to this book are **activities**—for the site staff developing the themes and thematic tours (part 1) and for the guides who are trained to give these new tours (part 2). By learning, doing, and interacting, staff and guides will become actively engaged in interpreting their site. This will enliven the planning and training process, which in turn will enliven the visitor's experience. Tours that combine well-researched and engaging information, strong themes, and an enthusiastic presentation assure vivid and positive memories for visitors.

A thematic tour is filled with the life and significance of the site and it is memorable for visitors. With this training, Mrs. Dodge will learn the benefits and pleasure of giving a *thematic tour* of the Caleb Crawley house. Her public will be delighted and remember their visit for all the right reasons.

Welcome to the Caleb Crawley House! I hope you will enjoy your visit to a very special place. Let me tell you just a bit about Mr. Crawley as we walk toward his home, the most elegant brick house in its day. Mr. Crawley was involved with local politics and was an early supporter of American independence. He had a model farm that Washington and Jefferson admired. He and his wife Elizabeth raised their four children here and there were also many servants and farmhands who tended the fields. This was a pretty lively place two hundred years ago! If you will step this way, we'll head for the house so we can get an idea of what life was like here. . . .

PART ONE

DEVELOPING THE THEMATIC TOUR

What Is a Thematic Tour? A Summary

Thematic tours link information—facts, ideas, and stories—in ways that help people understand and remember what they have heard and seen. *Thematic tours* emphasize and reinforce the most important historical messages of a site. *Thematic tours* do not tell visitors every single fact. Rather, they are more like a short story with a clearly articulated plot that has a beginning, middle, and logical conclusion. Excellent illustrations—the site's physical resources—visually reinforce the story's plot and help people remember key information. Thematic tours offer a presentation strategy that makes it easier, more interesting, and even entertaining for visitors who come to learn *and* to have fun. A carefully constructed tour presented engagingly by a knowledgeable guide helps assure that visitors have a pleasant experience and that they will remember something important about the site. ***Developing a thematic tour* requires hard but satisfying work by the staff and others associated with the site.**

Thematic tours require the following components:

- A descriptive **storyline** that summarizes the most historically significant information about the site.
- Three to five **themes** that illustrate the storyline.
- **Physical evidence**, specifically the site's material culture: architecture, collections, and landscape.
- Well-researched **short biographies** of significant people associated with the site. Like the physical evidence, the *real people* who lived and worked at the site make its story distinctive and human.
- **Historical context,** or background information, that visitors need to know to understand the site's themes and storyline.
- A **thematic tour outline** organized around the site's storyline, themes, physical evidence, biographies, and historical context. This outline creates a structure that links information, ideas, and the physical evidence of the site in a coherent way. A tour carefully built around a thematic tour outline will help visitors understand and remember what they have seen and heard at a historic site.

More complete descriptions and examples of each of these components may be found in Reading 2.1, *Storylines, Themes, Physical Evidence, Biographies, and Historical Context,* and Reading 3.1, *Storylines, Themes, Physical Evidence, Biographies, and Historical Context: Pulling It All Together* (pp. 23 and 43).

Introduction

HISTORIC SITES, LIKE MUSEUMS OF ALL SIZES AND TYPES, SHARE the dual mission of preservation of their collections and educational service to the public. The preservation component of a historic site's mission is critical and of the highest priority. A museum is entrusted with the care of all kinds of interesting and important objects—in perpetuity. Few would dispute that a site must spend the time and money required to keep a roof tight, build secure storage shelves for a collection of ceramics, or conserve an important but badly cracked painting. Sophisticated advances in conservation have aided preservation efforts, as have grant-funded projects, scientific articles on preservation, curatorial workshops, and the emergence of a group of experts trained in museum-related disciplines. Preservation of a museum's collections is essential.

But what of the second part of an institution's mission: educating the general public and providing them access to the historic site? How does an institution present or *interpret* its distinctive collections to visitors?

Many museums and historic sites offer the public self-guided tours. In these situations, visitors travel at their own pace, as they experience the historic village, garden, battlefield, or exhibition.

> Some sites, especially those with heavy visitation, station guides in each room or other exhibited space to serve as both security and as an interpreter for the public. Stationed guides may demonstrate a task such as cooking or sewing, or they may simply offer a few words of explanation. They present *one piece* of the site's history to the public, rather than the full experience expected of the guided tour. Though this book primarily addresses the development of thematic guided tours, led by one person from beginning to end, many of the ideas and activities can be adapted at sites that use station tours.

Many historic sites in the United States, however, have chosen the guided tour as the primary method to share their resources with the public. To some extent this is a function of security. This applies in particular to historic houses, which are relatively small spaces filled with objects placed in a naturalistic display intended to suggest a past way of life. Unless these period room arrangements are exhibited behind protective barriers, a self-guided tour risks violation of the institution's mission to preserve its collections. *Guided tours* through these spaces therefore are often required as well as desirable, given the institution's responsibility to care for the objects entrusted to it.

Beyond the issue of security, guided tours have long served historic sites as an important way to communicate information on a *personal* level, from an enthusiastic guide to a fascinated visitor. Costumed ladies, for example, told thousands of visitors about the family heirlooms exhibited in a recreated colonial kitchen at the Philadelphia Centennial Exposition of 1876. This notion of a special person explaining historic objects carried through the early twentieth century, when numerous historical societies, historic sites and house museums, and the National Park Service were created. Guides, in mobcaps or Smokey Bear hats, led people through log cabins, antebellum mansions, presidential homes, forts, and historically significant public buildings. Whether at Monticello, the White House, the Alamo, or the oldest house in town, the guided tour has become embedded in the expectations of visitors *and* historic sites alike.

Given the popularity of guided tours, historic sites must devote time and care to the development of **tour content** and **guide training**. Moreover, no matter how strong their training program and their tours, all sites benefit from periodic review of their visitors' experiences.

This book offers a strategy by which sites can improve tour content and guide training. The first step is for sites to examine the tour they currently offer with the goal of strengthening it, specifically by developing a **thematic tour**. A thematic tour offers sites the opportunity to identify the key messages it wants visitors to learn and understand. A thematic tour is built on the site's most significant resources—its architecture, collections, research materials, historical context, and the life stories of those who lived, worked, and visited there. It then

There are many other ways to experience the resources of a historic site and it is important that sites develop a menu of offerings to engage audiences. Options include, but are not limited to,

exhibitions on special topics related to the primary themes discussed at the site;
self-guided tours of the landscape and outbuildings aided by brochures, labels, or signs;
special programs, such as lectures, hands-on demonstrations, or family days; and
school programs that link site themes with age-appropriate curricula.

Still, the guided tour geared to a general or specific audience remains the primary means of reaching the public at many historic sites.

distills this information and organizes it into a cohesive, strong **story** that people will enjoy and remember. A thematic tour does not overwhelm visitors with myriad and often disconnected facts. Rather, it develops a story that is well-researched, carefully constructed, and engaging. Well-trained guides, steeped in the site's historical significance and its distinctive physical evidence, deliver this story. Thematic tours are informative. They also connect with the public by establishing strong links and comparisons with contemporary life, interests, and experiences.

This recommendation—developing and then giving thematic tours—is built on sound educational theory as well as tested practice. The concept underlying the thematic tour is rooted in the fact that human beings have complex brains, different learning styles, and diverse personal experiences. Despite this, there are certain strategies that enhance learning for most people. A tour that is designed to take advantage of these strategies—while providing for the wide variety of learning styles, experience, and personal interests—has the best chance of success.

WHY THEMATIC TOURS WORK

The most effective, *memorable* learning often occurs when we are asked to focus on a few important **big ideas** that serve as an umbrella for smaller, related ideas. A good teacher, for example, may begin a lesson by saying, "Today you will learn these three things." After citing and explaining the three ideas, the teacher will expound upon them, ask questions, solicit ideas, or offer an activity that amplifies the three ideas she wants her class to learn, and more important, *remember*. Before the class leaves, she may conclude by repeating the three big ideas she wants everyone to take with them.

This teaching strategy, when employed creatively and dynamically, is extraordinarily effective because it focuses on a few big ideas, then uses these ideas as umbrellas to group related information and illustrations. It also provides the opportunity to repeat the key ideas several times. When done creatively, this process is easy to follow because it is organized and reinforces memory of the major concepts.

Historic sites can apply these principles of thematic focus, grouping, and creative repetition to develop tours that maximize and enhance visitors' experiences. Rather than tell visitors *everything* there is to know about a site, sites should focus on the information they truly want visitors to remember. This often requires hard choices, but good interpretation requires figuring out both what to say *and* what *not* to say. Most people remember best when they hear a few, well-delivered ideas. How many ideas are a "few"? Most sites will find that **three to five significant ideas or *themes* typically work best. When these themes are woven together, they provide a *storyline* that is a succinct, yet compelling summary of the important ideas, events, and features that make a site special.**

As will be explained later in this chapter, *themes* are not simply facts. Themes incorporate facts to articulate a significant message. As an example, it is a *fact* that the Declaration of Independence was written in 1776. A *theme* built on that fact might be: *The Declaration of Independence, written in 1776, transformed the American colonies into a young nation that fought for its freedom.* **Another way to say it is that a theme explains why a fact is worth remembering.**

Identifying, then incorporating strong themes into a guided tour helps a site define the story it wants to share with the public. This book is designed to help sites identify their most important themes and write a strong storyline. These tasks lie at the heart of new thematic guided tours that identify and reinforce the site's significance. Crafting an excellent guided tour—a *thematic* tour—is an essential ingredient for strengthening the impact of the site. It will aid the site and its guides in creating an enjoyable experience for visitors. Ultimately, an excellent tour is a good product that will potentially attract new visitors.

Sam Ham, a leader in the interpretation of parks and the environment, offers a good guideline in his book, *Environmental Interpretation.* Drawing on research in human cognition, Ham states,

> Research has shown that the sheer amount of information, as well as how it's organized, make a difference in how well we're able to sort it out and use it. Studies have shown that most people are capable of handling about "7 ± 2" different pieces of information at a time. That is, some people can keep as many as nine different ideas or facts straight in their heads, whereas others can only deal with five or fewer. This relationship has less to do with the person's intelligence than it does with the amount of prior experience he or she has with the topic at hand. It stands to reason, then, that since some people in your audiences will have difficulty when the number exceeds five, you should limit the number of main ideas in your presentation to five or fewer. Doing so will make it easier for people in your audience to follow your ideas, and this will increase the likelihood that they'll continue paying attention to you. (Sam Ham, *Environmental Interpretation: A Practical Guide for People with Big Ideas and Small Budgets* [Golden, Colo.: Fulcrum, 1992], p. 22.)

By following the sequence of steps described in part 1, site staff can identify and produce **the components needed to develop the thematic tour.** Creating a strong thematic tour requires staff time and some expense in the short run. The long-term benefits, however, are incalculable if visitors enjoy and learn from their tour, and recommend it to others. The process of developing thematic tours can also help define the overall interpretive mission of a site, potentially influencing the thrust of the site's future special programs, exhibits, videos, and school curricula. The step-by-step process that follows is essential to building a strong thematic tour. By employing this process, a site will identify key *topics,* that can be developed into interpretive *themes,* which can be linked to create an overall *storyline* that is memorable and interesting. Once this is accomplished, sites will be poised to employ the guide training strategy outlined in part 2.

Beyond Commemoration: How Good Research, Probing Questions, and Strong (Even Provocative) Themes Enrich Historical Interpretation

Good historical interpretation is much more than presenting a collection of static facts and unchanging objects. The best historical interpretation examines a topic, idea, event, or person from many perspectives and asks a variety of provocative questions.

As Freeman Tilden wrote in *Interpreting Our Heritage*, good interpretation requires using all kinds of evidence to convey meaning and significance. To move beyond commemoration, historic sites are increasingly presenting more complex, multidimensional stories of the events and people that make them special. This may involve examining how issues such as race, gender, and class played out in the history of the site. This likely will broaden a site's interpretation to include the "voices" of people whose experiences are seldom and maybe never addressed: slaves on an antebellum plantation, workers in factories, servants, children, and others far from the seat of power, whether of a household or a government. Race, gender, and class are issues, too, that resonate with contemporary audiences and our experiences as twenty-first-century Americans.

Adding these voices to a site's interpretation may require tackling subjects that can seem difficult. For example, when admiring the architecture of a grand estate, a guide may be uncomfortable discussing how its owner amassed great wealth by running a factory that required workers to toil twelve hours a day for low wages in deplorable conditions.

Developing a multidimensional interpretation of a site that addresses sensitive or controversial topics can seem risky at first. In fact, though, taking risks implies seizing opportunities to expand knowledge and experience. Historic sites must be willing to take risks and present an interpretation that is balanced and honest, because in the end that makes the past meaningful for contemporary visitors.

If a site identifies themes that have sensitive components, guides must be well-prepared and comfortable in presenting this information. See chapter 7, Activities 7.6 and 7.7, for training that can help accomplish this.

CHAPTER 1

Preparation: *Assemble the Facts*

FACTS AND INFORMATION ARE THE BUILDING BLOCKS REQUIRED to develop the key *ideas* or *themes* about the site and its historical significance. Most sites are awash with all kinds of facts and information, which accumulated over time and in different formats. To develop a strong thematic interpretation of a site, staff should identify the most accurate and informative written materials that are available. These materials should be placed in an accessible location for the duration of the thematic tour development process. In addition, members of the theme development team should receive notebooks with photocopies of core materials that they will be expected to read before the roundtable workshop. (Similar notebooks will be needed for guides trained with the activities found in part 2).

The site should assemble the following materials for the notebooks.

Mission statement: A mission statement identifies the purpose and goals of the historic site and is typically codified by a board of directors. It may be general or quite specific. It is important that everyone associated with the site be familiar with its mission statement.

Site brochure: Most sites have a brochure or rack card that provides a brief summary of the history of the site and often includes illustrations or maps. It can be a short, handy reference when work on the tour begins. *Remember*: visitors take the brochure with them when they leave the site. During the tour development process, think about whether the brochure successfully presents the site to the public. If not, consider how the brochure might be changed.

Site history: Many sites have conducted research projects that have resulted in narrative histories of the site as a whole or particular aspects of the site. Overall histories should include what happened at the site—its people, architecture, landscape, significant events, and relationship with its neighborhood—over a considerable period of time. Topical studies might include an analysis of the architecture, or an in-depth study of a particular *event*, such as a battle, or *activity*, such as farming, milling, or carpentry. Be sure that information in the site history is correct and up to date. **If no concise site history is available, a staff member should prepare a three- to five-page synopsis that includes a discussion of the site's overall development, pertinent historical figures, important dates, significant events, and essential historical context. If there is an extensive site history, use the executive summary or create a three- to five-page synopsis.** A condensed summary of the site's history is essential when developing thematic tours and a guide training curriculum.

Time line: A time line is a particularly useful resource that lays out events from a site's history in tandem with relevant local, national, or international events. A time line is relatively easy to produce and aids the site's interpretation in significant ways, including in the development and implementation of thematic tours.

❖ *If a site lacks a time line, staff should prepare one prior to the roundtable workshop. The time line will also be used for guide training. An example may be found on p. 52 (Sample Material 3.1).*

Summary chart of the significant residents or other people associated with the site: This should include names, birth and death dates, and genealogical connections as needed. This chart should be brief—one page—and viewed as a handy reference to be used in conjunction with the time line and short biographies.

Short biographies: Many sites have one or more important historical figures connected with them. If published biographies exist, make them available to the staff and guides. However, to present a well-rounded interpretation of the site, it is important to know about the *other* people connected with it. Be sure to develop short biographies of the laborers (servants, slaves, skilled craftsmen, or workers), children, visitors, and others whose stories can add a variety of "real people" perspectives to the overall interpretation. Examples of this type of biography are found on *pp. 54–56* (Sample Material 3.2).

The resources listed below, often available at historic sites, can supplement the required materials cited above, or can be used to develop materials such as the site history and time line. Review the materials available at your site, select those that will be useful for theme development or guide training, and copy them for the participants' notebooks.

❖ *Most sites will have only some of these resources. Use this list to help identify as many written materials as possible. Even if your site does not have one of the formal documents cited, it may have certain components of that document. For example, very few sites have a historic landscape report, but many sites have a landscape plan or map that can be helpful for developing both thematic tours and guide training.*

Historic structures report (HSR): Many sites have conducted studies that result in a historic structures report. These typically are supervised by an architect or architectural historian and they focus on the site's buildings: the house, outbuildings, and other structures. The architect usually works with a team of experts who contribute to the overall report. The HSR team can include historians, paint analysts, structural engineers, and archaeologists. An HSR will include a detailed history of the buildings from construction through present conditions. Architectural drawings (elevations, floor plans, and architectural details) are usually done. A site plan or map is also often part of the scope of work. HSRs are filled with an enormous amount of information. For tour development, particularly useful excerpts include site plans and elevations, a building chronology, and the executive summary or summary history of the property.

Historic landscape report (HLR): A historic landscape report does for the site's landscape what an HSR does for its buildings. A landscape architect or cultural landscape historian typically supervises the study, with contributions being made by other historians, archaeologists, and horticulturists. The report should include overall site maps as well as detailed plans showing significant features, such as a formal garden. There should be a discussion of the different plant materials used at the site over time, including crops, trees, shrubs, and flowers. Sometimes HLRs, rather than HSRs, include information about outbuildings because they are essential built components of the landscape. Maps and the HLR executive summary can provide useful background.

Grant proposals: Sites often must prepare summary histories as part of grant applications. These can be useful introductions to the site's significance, mission, collections, and programs. Federal grant applications from the Institute for Museum and Library Services (IMLS), Museum Assessment Program (MAP), Conservation Assessment Program (CAP), and National Endowment for the Humanities (NEH) all require background narratives about the site. These materials can aid interpretive planning.

***Room books or room cards*:** Curatorial information about the objects in the collection—decorative arts, fine arts, manuscripts, and printed materials—offers important facts pertinent to the interpretation of the site. Collection objects are key components—the physical evidence—of a thematic tour. Room books or photocopies of registration materials for significant objects are critical resources for developing a thematic tour.

Archives: Many sites have important collections of manuscripts, photographs, maps, and other printed and written primary source materials that are integral to the site's history. A finding aid to these collections or photocopies of important examples can inform the development of the site's themes.

Furnishing plan: This document typically addresses the installation of period room spaces. It includes references to the specific objects displayed in the room and, usually, a discussion of the interpretive philosophy that guided the installation. For example, a furnishing plan for a late-nineteenth-century bedroom will address who the occupant was (age, socioeconomic status, etc.), the available documentation for the room (period inventories, primary and secondary resources), and the interpretive mission for the space (e.g., to show a representative bed chamber for a maid in a wealthy house). A furnishing plan reflects considerable research and thought. Consequently, it can be a useful tool in the tour development process.

***On-site library*:** Most historic sites assemble books, catalogues, magazines, and other printed materials on related topics in areas such as American history, decorative arts, industrial history, military or political history, social and cultural history, archaeology, horticulture, and architecture. These books offer important historical context for interpreting the site and should be made available for reference.

***Unpublished research*:** Site staff and students often conduct research about a particular aspect of the site. Short papers on topics such as Chinese export porcelain, the introduction of indoor plumbing, or the role of servants can offer important information. In addition, students at local schools or colleges occasionally do research papers or theses, again offering information with a particular focus. These materials should be reviewed for accuracy and pertinence to interpretive planning. A notebook containing relevant papers should be included on the reference shelf.

***Bibliography of additional primary and secondary sources*:** A good bibliography identifies sources of additional information about historical context or background relevant to the site's story. It also helps direct future research and planning. Creating a bibliography is often a good project for a motivated guide, an intern, or a student at a local school.

Market research, visitor surveys, and other materials that identify current and potential audiences: To serve the public well, historic sites must become familiar with their visitors' needs and expectations. Many museums have conducted surveys that identify crucial demographics, visitor interests, and reactions to tours and exhibits. If formal surveys exist, a site should assess this data and use it to inform plans for new thematic interpretation. Even if a site does not have a formal visitor survey or study, it can often retrieve helpful information. For example, many historic sites ask visitors to sign a guest log. This can be reviewed to obtain basic information about current visitation. Do most people come from out of town or are the majority "day trippers" who live relatively nearby? How many visitors come in large groups, such as a bus or school tour? Even this basic information can help shape the content, logistics, and presentation of a tour. If a site chooses to gather more information, it can devise questionnaires to distribute to willing visitors. These can further refine understanding of the demographics of current visitors and provide substantive knowledge about how they enjoyed the tour, what they were most interested in, and what recommendations they might have for improvements. Focus groups, generally conducted by consulting professionals, can serve the same purpose. Also consider talking with nearby cultural sites to swap information about audiences and call local convention and visitors bureaus, which typically have lots of data that will be of interest.

A site's **videos, exhibits, catalogues, newsletters or other publications, school programs,** and **yearly calendars of public programs** are important resources. Some provide useful background information; others offer a window on current interpretive efforts. The thematic tour team should be familiar with *all* their site's interpretive programs as part of developing strong thematic tours.

Theme Development Resources: A Checklist

Members of the theme development team will need a variety of resources to inform them about the site. A good guideline is to provide materials that will take two to three hours to read. (Budget this time for paid consultants.) This preparation will reduce the amount of time required for introductory comments at the roundtable and will assure that good planning begins immediately.

Here is a sample table of contents for background materials assembled for the Caleb Crawley House. Each member of the thematic tour team will receive these materials prior to the roundtable workshop.

*1. Mission statement
*2. Current brochure and current newsletter
*3. Three-page site history prepared by the site director
*4. A time line that cites the important dates for the Caleb Crawley House (architectural development, birth and death dates of significant residents, dates of significant events that occurred there, references to dates and events in American history)
*5. Summary chart of the significant residents of the site
*6. Short biographies of Caleb and Elizabeth Crawley, their son Benjamin, and their cook, Rachel
7. Several paragraphs excerpted from an Institute for Museum and Library Services grant that describe the site and its resources
8. A site map
9. A photocopy of a research paper prepared by a graduate student on the journals of Elizabeth Crawley
10. Photocopies of several pages from the journals of Elizabeth Crawley
11. A bibliography of key contextual history
12. Pertinent information about current visitation and, if available, information about target audiences that will expand visitation

*Must have these items.

CHAPTER 2

Planning: *The Theme Development Team and the Roundtable Workshop*

SOME HISTORIC SITES HAVE ENGAGED IN INTERPRETIVE PLANNING, and as part of that process have identified the key themes or interpretive messages that are central to the site's public programming. If a site has an interpretive plan that identifies its primary themes, it is ready to use them to develop a thematic tour outline (see chapter 3, *Creating: Writing, Revising, and Testing the Thematic Tour Outline*). If a tour outline has already been developed based on the primary themes, the site is ready to train guides to give thematic tours (see part 2).

If a site has *not* identified and clearly articulated its themes, it is essential that it do so before developing and implementing thematic tours. An effective, yet relatively efficient way to achieve this is for the site to conduct a series of structured discussions with staff and outside consultants. The activities that follow form the core for a one- or two-day **roundtable workshop** to help sites write the storyline and themes that will provide the interpretive foundation for new thematic tours. The roundtable workshop has four components: writing a draft **storyline** for the site, **identifying the important material culture and biographical evidence** for the site, **identifying the significant historical topics** associated with the site, and using all the material developed during this process to **develop and draft the main interpretive themes** for the site's new thematic tours.

Holding a **theme development roundtable workshop** requires four steps:

- Meet with site staff to set goals for developing and implementing interpretive, thematic guided tours and to name the staff member who will serve as project coordinator
- Identify members of the theme development team
- Set the schedule and prepare activities for the roundtable workshop
- Hold the roundtable workshop and its related activities.

> The roundtable workshop should not be viewed as interpretive planning for the site as a whole, as that process necessarily is more extensive. However, conversations spurred by the roundtable can offer useful background when a site *does* develop a comprehensive interpretive plan to address such issues as visitors' centers, exhibits, videos or other media projects, school programs, Web sites, promotional campaigns, publications, grant proposals, and special programs.

SITE STAFF PREPARATION

Once a site makes a general decision to upgrade its guided tours, staff members should spend time thinking, talking, and planning to assure a good result. One effective strategy is to hold several all-staff brainstorming sessions. Use the time together to discuss the current state of the guided tour at the site and consider new possibilities. Site staff typically brims with ideas and information. Think out loud and record the information on tape, as notes, or on flip-chart pages. Consider such questions as:

What messages or information does our site try to give visitors at the present time?

What messages does the visitor actually get? (Use visitor surveys if available)

What are the site's resources that make it special, both historically (ideas) and visually (physical evidence such as architecture, collections, and landscape)?

Which staff can provide information about particular aspects of the site's story? (Director? Archaeologist? Curator? Educator?) What resources can they contribute to the planning process? (Collections files? Research? Visitor surveys?)

What useful insights have staff members gleaned from previous work experiences or visits to other sites?

Are there sites nearby that give excellent guided tours and therefore would be worth visiting (both as a "tourist" and to speak with site staff)?

What are the best stories currently being told to visitors? The worst?

Do the current guided tours link well with other visitor experiences (videos, exhibits, programs, brochures, school tours, hands-on activities, etc.)? If not, what can be done to facilitate better meshing?

Will the current guiding staff be amenable to a new approach? If not, what will facilitate this?

What outside consultants might have useful knowledge or insight about the site?

Does the site have the time, money, personnel, energy, and desire to consider and execute new ideas? Specifically, is the site committed to creating and implementing new thematic tours with the overall goal of enhancing the interpretive mission?

❖ *Sites will need to allot time, talent, and money to improve guided tours. Without significant commitment by site staff, and by extension, the site's board of directors, it will be difficult to accomplish the work suggested in this book.*

These brainstorming sessions are a wonderful way to build staff enthusiasm about a crucial goal: delivering the best possible tour to the visiting public. With the staff working as a team, the planning and implementation process will proceed smoothly. The best plans are the product of many minds, not just one. A team process will also assure excellent communication and help prevent unexpected surprises.

Though developing new tours must be a team effort, one member of the staff should serve as the project coordinator. At larger sites, the educator or public services coordinator might be the logical choice. At smaller sites, the director may be the right person. The project coordinator must allocate considerable time to the project. Responsibilities include coordinating all aspects of the roundtable workshop, running the roundtable workshop, leading staff through the development of a new thematic tour outline, facilitating communication among the members of the planning team, and insuring that the remainder of the staff and board are kept informed.

IDENTIFYING THE THEME DEVELOPMENT TEAM

Developing themes for a site is best accomplished as a team process. Sites should assemble a diverse but knowledgeable group of people who are skilled in the interpretation of history and interested in planning thematic tours grounded in excellent research. Depending on the size of the site, the team can have as few as four or five people, or as many as eight or ten. The team must be big enough to allow for a range of expertise and opinions and small enough that the group can work together and reach a consensus.

After the site staff has met for their brainstorming session, the project coordinator should identify the members of the **theme development team**. ***Staff members*** to consider include the **director, curator, museum educator, public relations specialist, historian, and horticulturist.** Members of the **guiding staff** can offer invaluable insight about current and desired visitor experiences. A veteran guide who is open to change can provide the wisdom of experience. A newer guide can contribute fresh ideas. Either or both can ease the process of getting other guides to "buy in" to thematic tours and the additional training they will require. Guides who have been involved with the thematic tour planning process will also be invaluable as mentors to new guides, an important component of the training program presented in part 2. ***Board members*** **with useful professional expertise** are also potential members of the thematic tour team. Examples include an architect, a horticulturist, or a teacher.

It is important to have members of the team other than site staff, board members, and volunteers to provide an outsider's perspective. These team members will work as ***professional consultants*** and should be paid for their services. If possible, plan to pay the consultants for two or three days of work: one-half day to review materials sent to them, one or two days at the roundtable workshop, and one-half day to write a short report synthesizing their thoughts about interpretation at the site. Budget for consultants' fees, as well as travel and lodging expenses if they are required. It is often possible to obtain small planning grants from public or private sources that can cover these expenses as well as others associated with the development of the thematic tour.

Look for some consultants whose areas of expertise are strongly related to the history of the site and others whose skills are related to the needs of the process. Identify areas of strength within the staff where no additional expertise is needed. At the same time, identify those areas where outside assistance will be helpful and even crucial. For example, if the curator has a wealth of knowledge about nineteenth-century architecture, there is no need to seek an architectural historian for the thematic tour planning team. Conversely, if the staff has limited knowledge about an important feature of the site, whether a historical event or person, or important collection, it would be useful to include an expert who can address this issue. Potential thematic tour team consultants include:

- **Scholars or other experts with expertise in subjects linked to the major themes at the site**. Be sure the chosen scholarly fields have the potential to contribute in a significant way to the interpretation of the site and to provide valuable historical context. Avoid interesting but peripheral areas of study. Depending on the site, areas to consider include political, economic, and military history; women's studies; African American and Native American studies; horticultural and landscape history; the social, architectural, or economic history of the community where the site is located; and material culture and archaeology.
- **An interpretive specialist or museum educator** skilled in tour development and the specific strategies historic sites can employ to best deliver their historical messages to the public.

Include at least two outside consultants on the theme development team, and up to about five if the budget allows. If possible, find local experts to avoid travel and lodging costs. Local experts, too, carry the potential advantage of continuing their relationship as advisors to the site in the future. Colleges and universities can be helpful in identifying experts. So too can state humanities councils or other regional historic preservation agencies. Finally, staff at other historic sites may know experts and scholars who could contribute to thematic tour planning.

Planning the Roundtable Workshop: Checklist of Preparations

Site staff, led by the project coordinator, should establish the **schedule** for each step of the planning process: the **initial brainstorming sessions**, the date(s) for the **roundtable workshop**, and the **staff time required to develop a new thematic tour outline**. Guide training, using the strategy presented in part 2, must also be scheduled. Place all of these dates and time commitments on the overall site calendar to prevent conflicts.

The Project Coordinator should:

- Identify and notify members of the theme development team.
- Prepare a budget.
- Set a date for the roundtable workshop and contact all team members. Encourage their questions about appropriate preparation.
- Before the date, send notebooks containing the photocopied materials described in chapter 1 to all participants. Request that all team members review these materials prior to the roundtable workshop.
- Plan where to hold the roundtable. Hold it on the site, if possible, so participants have easy access to the historic resources. If the site lacks good meeting space, and the roundtable would be more comfortably accomplished elsewhere, be sure that the outside consultants have already seen the site.
- Provide ample refreshment. Coffee, tea, sodas, lunch, and snacks will keep people happy and focused.
- Assemble the materials needed for the roundtable activities: flip charts, an easel, paper, extra pens, 3 × 5 cards, and a tape recorder and tapes to record the proceedings. Consider including additional resources such as an orientation video and the equipment needed to show it.

IMPORTANT: Read through the activities designed for the roundtable workshop, practice them, and be prepared to lead them on the day of the roundtable.

❖ *In some instances it may be preferable for someone other than the project coordinator to run the roundtable workshop. This role may be filled by another staff member or a consultant. Whoever leads the workshop will need to work closely with the project coordinator to be certain that the roundtable goals are met.*

Sample Budget Line Items: Theme Development Roundtable Workshop at the Caleb Crawley House

Personnel

Staff time

Project coordinator (lead staff member)
- 1 day staff brainstorming session
- 10 days preparation
- 1–2 days roundtable
- 3 days wrap up
- 1 day staff meeting to create thematic tour outline
- 1 day, total, piloting and revising the outline

Curator
- 1 day staff brainstorming session
- 1 day total, pre- and postroundtable work
- 1–2 days roundtable
- 1 day staff meeting to create thematic tour outline
- 1 day, total, piloting and revising the outline

Museum educator
- 1 day staff brainstorming session
- 1 day total, pre- and postroundtable work
- 1–2 days roundtable
- 1 day staff meeting to create thematic tour outline
- 1 day, total, piloting and revising the outline

Public relations specialist
- 1 day staff brainstorming session
- 1 day total, pre- and postroundtable work
- 1–2 days roundtable
- 1 day staff meeting to create thematic tour outline
- 1 day, total, piloting and revising the outline

Veteran guide(s)
- 1 day staff brainstorming session
- 1 day total, pre- and postroundtable work
- 1–2 days roundtable
- 1 day staff meeting to create thematic tour outline
- 1 day, total, piloting and revising the outline

Board member/architect
- 1 day total, pre- and postroundtable work
- 1–2 days roundtable

Consultant time

Consultant 1
- 1 day total, pre- and postroundtable work
- 1–2 days roundtable

Consultant 2
1 day total, pre- and postroundtable work
1–2 days roundtable

Consultant 3
1 day total, pre- and postroundtable work
1–2 days roundtable

❖ *Extra money should be budgeted if consultants are from out of town and require transportation, lodging, and food.*

Materials

On-site facilities
meeting space, tables, and chairs
photocopy machine and paper
tape recorder to tape proceedings

Purchased materials
easel, flip charts, and markers
notebooks
scratch pads and pens
3×5 cards
postage
refreshments for roundtable
tapes and tape recorder

The Roundtable Workshop: Goals, Schedule, and Activities

The ***goal*** of the roundtable workshop is to develop new themes for the site in order to design a new thematic tour. To facilitate the process, the roundtable should follow a structure built around a series of four activities intended to identify the storyline and themes for the site. These four activities are:

- **Summarizing the Site's Significance on an Index Card**
- **Material Culture and Biography in a Historic House Setting**
- **Identifying the Site's Topics**
- **Writing the Site's Themes**

The activities are not difficult and should stimulate lively discussion as well as a focused approach. Aim for a roundtable in which *everyone* contributes and the end product reflects the ideas of many coalesced into a shared vision. Allow time for brainstorming and for refreshment: both help fuel creative juices. Be sure to tape the proceedings for future reference.

Two sample schedules follow. The first is for a two-day roundtable, the recommended strategy, as it permits longer discussion and a more comprehensive approach. The second is for a compressed one-day roundtable that, though less desirable, may be necessary for sites on a limited budget.

Sample Schedule: Roundtable Workshop to Develop Thematic Tours at the Caleb Crawley House (Two Days)

Day One

8:30–9 A.M.	— ***Coffee and informal conversation***
9–9:30	— **Welcome and introduction** to the site by the director and/or project coordinator. If the site has an orientation video, show it. If the site does not, plan to spend a few minutes giving some background about the site's history and the organization that runs it. State that the purpose of the roundtable is to develop themes on which an improved tour will be based.
9:30–11	— **Site tour** led by a veteran guide or staff member.
11–11:15	— ***Coffee break***
11:15–12:30 P.M.	— **Initial reactions**: Have each member of the team *briefly* state their pertinent experience, area of expertise, and perspective on your historic site. Ask each person to offer a few thoughts about the site and the tour experience.
12:30–1:30	— ***Lunch break***
1:30–2:15	— **Activity 1:** *Summarizing the Site's Significance on an Index Card*
2:15–2:30	— **Discussion**
2:30–2:45	— ***Coffee (or cold drink) break***
2:45–3:45	— **Activity 2:** *Material Culture and Biography in a Historic House Setting*
3:45–4:30	— **Wrap-up discussion and comments**

Day Two

9:30–9:45 A.M.	— **Comments, thoughts about day one**
9:45–11	— **Activity 3:** *Identifying the Site's Topics*
11–11:15	— ***Coffee break***
11:15–12:30 P.M.	— **Activity 4:** *Identifying the Site's Themes*
12:30–1:30	— ***Lunch break***
1:30–3:30	— **Comments and ideas. Wrap-up discussion, assignments (if necessary), and thanks to all for their hard work!** By the conclusion of the roundtable, site staff will have draft versions of a new storyline for the site, the key three to five themes illustrated at the site and well-identified locations on the site that illustrate the themes and storyline. With this information staff can begin building an outline for a thematic tour.

Sample Schedule: Roundtable Workshop to Develop Thematic Tours at the Caleb Crawley House (One Day)

8:30–9 A.M.	— ***Coffee and informal conversation***
9–9:20	— **Welcome and introduction**
9:30–10:30	— **Site tour** led by a veteran guide or staff member
10:30–10:45	— ***Coffee break***
10:45–11:45	— **Initial reactions**
11:45–12:30 P.M.	— **Activity 1:** *Summarizing the Site's Significance on an Index Card*
12:30–1:30	— ***Lunch break***
1:30–2:30	— **Activity 2:** *Material Culture and Biography in a Historic House Setting*
2:45–4:00	— **Activity 3:** *Identifying the Site's Topics*
4:00–4:15	— ***Coffee (or cold drink) break***
4:15–5:30	— **Activity 4:** *Identifying the Site's Themes*
5:30–6:00	— **Wrap-up discussion, assignments (if necessary), and thanks to all for their hard work!**

ROUNDTABLE WORKSHOP ACTIVITIES

Summarizing the Site's Significance on an Index Card—The Storyline

Purpose: To begin to identify the primary story of the historic site.

Time: Forty-five minutes

Preparation: Assemble materials

- Photocopy of Reading 2.1, *Storylines, Themes, Physical Evidence, Biographies, and Historical Context,* for each participant
- Blank 3 × 5 card for each participant
- Flip chart and markers

Procedure:

1. Distribute Reading 2.1, *Storylines, Themes, Physical Evidence, Biographies, and Historical Context.* Give the participants a few minutes to read it. Open a discussion about what a storyline is. Emphasize that a storyline summarizes what is important and memorable about your historic site. Describe it as being similar to the plot synopsis for a movie or short story and as having a coherent sequence and narrative thread. State that it will underpin all forms of interpretation at the site, including guided tours, publications, special programs and events, and multimedia presentations.
2. Ask each participant to review the site history and the site brochure, both of which are included in their notebooks. Encourage them to highlight or underline those ideas they consider most important.
3. Write "[name of site] tells the story of . . . " on the flip chart. Give each person a 3 × 5 card and ask them to use it to complete the sentence. Encourage them to think about what they have read, then spend ten to fifteen minutes writing a few sentences expressing the ideas they have decided are most important. The statements should be no longer than one side of the 3 × 5 card. (Have extra cards available if people need them for revisions.)
4. When everyone has finished, ask each person, one by one, to read what they have written. Record the main ideas cited by the group on the flip chart, two or three per page, leaving space between them. If ideas are repeated or overlap, make a mark to indicate this.
5. Review the assembled list and open a discussion. Has anything been omitted? What key ideas keep reappearing?
6. Review, discuss, and revise the lists of ideas. Identify the most frequently mentioned pieces of the site's story. Circle these on the chart.
7. Lead a wrap-up discussion and conclude by stating that the group has identified key ideas that can be developed later by the site staff into a polished storyline.

❖ *The project coordinator should collect the 3 × 5 cards and save the flip chart pages for reference when the staff works to write a polished storyline for the site (see chapter 3).*

Storylines, Themes, Physical Evidence, Biographies, and Historical Context

Definitions and Examples

A good interpretive experience includes a carefully organized message that helps visitors learn what is important about a historic site. Good interpretive experiences, no matter what their form, share four organizing elements:

- a clear and concise **storyline**
- three to five **themes** that convey the most important ideas about a site
- the **physical evidence** and **short biographies** that make a site special and illustrate its storyline and themes
- the pertinent **historical context** that visitors will need to know to get full benefit from the site's interpretation

It takes time to develop these components, but both the process and the end product will help define how a site can coordinate its tours, programs, and other forms of public outreach in ways that are educational, coherent, memorable, and even fun.

The Storyline

The **storyline** summarizes the fundamental story and significance of the historic site. A storyline follows a logical sequence with a beginning, middle, and conclusion, much like a short story or movie plot. In concise, clear language a storyline conveys the chief ideas that make a site important and memorable. It may be a few sentences or a few paragraphs, but no more than that. A good way to start thinking about a storyline is to finish the phrase, "[Name of your site] tells the story of. . . ." Another way to think about it is to ask, what does your site "say" or illustrate better than any place else? What is the distinctive "message" of your site?

Here is a sample storyline developed for the (fictional) Caleb Crawley House.

> **The Caleb Crawley House tells the story of a family devoted to American independence before, during, and after the Revolutionary War.** Caleb Crawley, trained in law but a farmer by preference, was an early and outspoken opponent of King George's authority. He tried to rally his neighbors to support tea and stamp boycotts but was arrested in 1773 for his activities. While Caleb was under arrest, his wife Elizabeth ran the farm, often helping her farm hands plow the fields. She wrote passionate letters to her imprisoned husband, declaring her determination that both the farm and American freedom succeed. During the Revolution both Caleb and his son Benjamin served in the Continental army. Elizabeth kept a journal during this period, offering a remarkable window on the lives of her family at a significant moment in American history. With independence and peace, Caleb returned to the beautiful brick house and farm he loved, Elizabeth devoted herself to her garden, and their sons went on to found textile mills that were among the first steam-powered industries in America.

Themes

A **theme** expresses an important idea interpreted at the site. Themes emerge from the storyline and convey messages you want visitors to remember, much like people remember the "moral of a story" in a short story or movie. A theme is not a single word or fact. Rather, a theme develops an important idea into a full sentence or two. Here are three themes derived from the storyline for the Caleb Crawley House. They come directly from the storyline, but are succinct enough for interpreters and visitors to remember.

1. **The Caleb Crawley family were staunch patriots who believed in American freedom.** Caleb Crawley was an early patriot who yearned to be a farmer yet went to jail for his beliefs. Elizabeth Crawley was a fiercely independent woman who ran the farm and wrote with eloquence. Caleb and Benjamin Crawley fought for freedom by joining the Continental army. Rachel Jones,

the cook who worked for the Crawley family for many years, was equally passionate about freedom. She was born a slave and, by hard work and careful saving, purchased her freedom in 1773.

2. **Eighteenth-century Americans had distinctive patterns of work, education, and socialization.** Responsibilities, duties, and opportunities were divided by class and gender. Wealthy families enjoyed advantages that ranged from better education to better food, clothing, and houses. Servants, slaves, indentured servants, craftsmen, and laborers did the largest part of the hard physical labor required to keep farms and other businesses going. However, the disruption of the Revolution forced changes. Men of all classes joined the military, leaving women behind to keep farms and businesses alive.

3. **Energetic individualism is a bedrock of American independence.** The Caleb Crawley House and its family offer representative examples of America's entrepreneurial spirit. The Crawleys boycotted tea, embraced the Jeffersonian ideal of a model farm, and invested in new industries. Their cook Rachel helped establish an important American institution, the African Methodist Episcopal Church.

Physical Evidence

A historic site by definition includes a wealth of physical evidence connected with its historical messages. This evidence includes the buildings, the landscape and its related outbuildings, and the collections of three-dimensional objects and two-dimensional manuscripts, maps, photographs, and paintings. The physical evidence makes historic sites special and should be the memorable illustration of the story presented during a guided tour. Physical evidence can be important in and of itself—for example, the original Declaration of Independence or Edison's first light bulb. People love to see the "real thing" and thematic tours of historic sites should satisfy this enthusiasm. This physical evidence is the *visible* documentation of a site's history and it conveys powerful visual information. Thematic tours must weave oral messages with visual messages to create a seamless interpretation that appeals to visitors of different ages, interests, and learning styles.

Short Biographies

History offers the story of human experiences over time. Historic sites tell the stories of particular people who lived, worked, visited, or waged war there, and they offer a window on the past. Human stories, or historical biographies, bring a historic site to life. If physical evidence helps the visitor visualize the site's interpretive messages, historical biographies are the essential site-specific counterpoints that humanize this same message. It is important, therefore, that a historic site conduct good research, then develop strong biographies of the various people connected with it. This is good history. It is also good interpretation, because most people love "people stories."

For example, a highly detailed description of the military history of the Revolutionary War would bore many visitors touring sites in Boston, Lexington, or Concord. An energized, well-documented account of the heroic ride of Paul Revere in April 1775, however, *personalizes* Boston's experience during the early years of the war. If told effectively, Paul Revere's story can serve to capture the danger and strong feelings held by *real people* that ultimately led to the first shots fired at Lexington.

Biographies need not be heroic, however, to offer strong interpretive possibilities. If a site's research has yielded information about the servants who worked there, a discussion of the kitchen will be more interesting and memorable if presented from the *perspective* of the cook. Rather than present an inventory of cooking utensils, good interpretation of this essential space might begin by saying,

> By 6 A.M., Rachel stoked the fire so that she could begin preparing the hominy, ham, and hot bread that the Crawley family would eat for breakfast later that morning.

Information about a *real person*, the cook Rachel, introduces a historic human presence in an interpreted space. Excellent research leading to excellent historical biographies will make historic sites places where real people lived and where real people will want to visit. The best thematic tours weave together the stories of a variety of people who lived on, worked at, or visited the site.

Historical Context

Identifying pertinent historical background is essential to assure that visitors understand the significance of the site. This **historical context** provides the related information that adds perspective to the history. A good way to think about this is to consider those relatively contemporary events that shape our own lives, *our* historical context. Examples of *historical context* topics that have influenced many Americans and American society today include

the Vietnam War
the assassination of John F. Kennedy
Neil Armstrong's walk on the moon
rock-and-roll music
computers
the civil rights and women's rights movements
immigration from Asia and Latin America

Knowledge of context, so vibrant in its own day, can fade over time. The past often appears to be a foreign country, a place and time that are remote from the lives we lead today. Identifying and reconstructing the historical context that shaped the lives of people who lived long ago rounds out the site's story and makes it more accurate. The particulars of historical context also can be used to connect lives of the past with those of the present. Historical events that offer potential context for a historic site could include

the Revolutionary War
Lincoln's assassination and its impact
driving the spike that linked the Union Pacific and the Central Pacific railroads
jazz
the invention and general use of the light bulb
the abolition movement
immigration from Central and Eastern Europe

These particular events can also be used to draw parallels with the modern examples, above.

Material Culture and Biography in a Historic House Setting

Purpose: To begin using the site's material culture as essential evidence for developing the site's major themes.

Time: Sixty minutes

Preparation: Assemble materials

Photocopies, Worksheet 2.1, *Using Material Culture and Biography to Interpret Historic Sites*, and Worksheet 2.2, *Using Material Culture and Biography to Build an Interpretive Tour*

Select five to six objects, each in a different historic space at the site. (If possible, choose a variety of media that reflects the site's collections of decorative arts, fine arts, and archives.) Choose obvious objects that illustrate important ideas about the site.

Procedure:

1. Divide the roundtable workshop participants into groups. Assign each group one object, in situ, in the historic space. Tell participates they will have twenty minutes to:

   A. *Examine* the assigned object, then complete Worksheet 2.1.

   B. *Consider* the object within its physical context, then complete Worksheet 2.2, which asks the following questions:

   - What is the relationship of this object to its room or exterior setting?
   - What does it "say" about that space and the historic people who once occupied it?
   - How can the object be used to interpret the site and its important stories to the public?

   C. *Prepare* a short, two- to three-minute interpretation of the space using the object and a historic character associated with it as a key illustration of a significant story about the site.

   Take each group to their particular room or exterior space and identify the object they will examine. Float among the groups as they work and answer questions as needed.

2. Reconvene the whole team. Moving sequentially around the property, have each group make its presentation. (Progress from exterior sites to interior spaces, using a path that mirrors a typical tour route.) After each mini-tour, encourage comments and questions.

3. Return to the meeting space. Encourage a brief wrap-up discussion. Collect the completed worksheets to use as reference when developing the site's topics, themes, and thematic tour outline.

Using Material Culture and Biography to Interpret Historic Sites

1. **What is this object?** *(Identification)*

2. **What does this object do? How was it used?** *(Function)*

3. **Who made, owned, used, and maintained this object?** *(People)*

4. **What are the relationships among the object, its function, and the people associated with it?** *(Ideas)*

5. **How has the use or knowledge of this object changed over time?**
   How can we use it to interpret larger stories of change over time?
   How can we use it to link past experiences with present-day realities?
   (Interpretation that links material culture and historic people with contemporary life)

Using Material Culture and Biography to Build an Interpretive Tour

With the information compiled in Worksheet 2.1, examine your object in its setting and answer these questions. Using short phrases or a list of key ideas is fine. Use the back if needed.

1. What is the relationship of this object to its room or exterior setting?

2. How can this object be used to interpret the space it is in?

3. How can this object be used to tell a story about a particular historic character associated with the site?

4. How can the story of this object and its associated historic person contribute to the overall interpretation of the site?

5. Prepare a two- to three-minute interpretation of this historic space using the object and the person associated with it as key illustrations of a significant theme or story. If possible, try to tell this story from the *perspective* of the person who used this object, using either first-person or third-person language.

Identifying the Site's Topics

Purpose: To begin identifying the key *topics* that reinforce the site's storyline. A topic is a noun, fact, or phrase that captures the gist of an idea.

Time: Seventy-five minutes

Preparation: Assemble materials
- Flip chart pages developed during Activity 2.1 (tape to walls or make available for people to see)
- Easel, flip chart, and markers of at least four colors

Procedure:

1. Introduce this activity by saying the group will develop a long list of *topics* that relate to the ideas that emerged during Activity 2.1, *Summarizing the Site's Significance on an Index Card.* Explain that a topic is a noun or a succinct phrase unembellished by descriptions or additional information. Illustrate the definition by referring to topics cited on the flip chart pages from Activity 2.1. (Some *topics* related to the Caleb Crawley House are the *Revolutionary War, the new republic, Georgian architecture, women's education in the eighteenth century, servants and slaves, American individualism, the birth of American manufacturing,* and *Chinese export porcelain.*)

2. Ask everyone to review their notes from Activity 2.1, the site time line in their notebooks, and the ideas generated by Activity 2.2. After a few minutes, initiate a brainstorming session to cite additional topics related to the site, noting these on a clean flip-chart page. Encourage a long list, but as ideas slow or when topics begin to overlap, end the discussion.

   ❖ *If a site's history includes sensitive topics, such as slavery, Native American relations, child labor, death, divorce, mental health, or difficult family relations, be sure they are listed. Encourage some brainstorming about effective ways to interpret these topics to the general public.*

3. Ask the group to review the long list of topics they have developed. Encourage questions and comments about whether the list as a whole reflects important pieces of the historical significance and story of the site. Revise the topics as needed.

4. Ask the team to look at the long list of topics. Open a discussion by saying that it is important for the site to prioritize topics by importance to the site's interpretation. Look at *each* topic. Make decisions that will shape priorities. Say that some topics will be *crucial*, others important but less central, and still others fairly minor. As a group, decide which topics are

   Crucial. Give these topics a number **"1."**

   Decide which topics are

   Important but less crucial. Give these topics a number **"2."**

   Decide which topics are

   Peripheral. Give these topics a number **"3."**

   ❖ *Certain topics will be crucial, such as the Revolutionary War for the Caleb Crawley House. Other topics may be more subtle, but will have potential interpretive significance, for example, education of women in the eighteenth century and related topics in women's history. Other topics likely will seem less important for a general audience and so might lose their rank in a prioritized list. Again, an example for the Caleb Crawley House might be Chinese export porcelain, if considered solely as a way to identify particular objects.*

Remember: *it is likely that more visitors will be interested in the* story *of the Caleb Crawley family—their patriotism, their daily lives, their accomplishments—than in a tour devoted to identifying the characteristics of the Chinese export porcelain found in the collection. (This type of tour is best suited for those with specialized interests in decorative arts.)*

5. Conclude by encouraging people to reach a consensus on those topics that are most important and on which the site should focus. Indicate these critical topics, marking them with a star.
6. Ask a member of the group to assist in making clean flip-chart pages that list two or three critical topics on each, leaving a space for writing beneath each topic.

Identifying the Site's Themes

Purpose: To help participants identify and prioritize themes for the site.

Time: Seventy-five minutes

Preparation: Assemble materials

Flip-chart pages of critical site *topics* prepared in Activity 2.3 (see step 6). Tape these to a wall or otherwise make them visible to the group

Photocopy Worksheet 2.3, *Outline: Using Sentences, Historical Context, Biographies, and Physical Evidence to Build Themes*

Flip chart and markers

Scratch paper

Optional: three colors of stick-on colored dots (one of each color per person)

Procedure:

1. Introduce this activity by telling the group that they will now turn each *topic* identified in Activity 2.3 into a *draft theme sentence* that expresses what is most important about that topic. Encourage the group to look at the many topics listed on the flip-chart pages hanging around the room. Explain that by turning each topic into a full sentence, they will identify precisely *what they want visitors to know about that topic*. This is the first step toward the development of a theme. Develop your own examples or use these sample topics for the Caleb Crawley House (Activity 2.3), expanded into fully developed *draft theme sentences.*

   The Revolutionary War marked the end of colonial America's dependence on Mother England and the beginning of national political and economic independence.

   Georgian architecture, prevalent during the Age of Reason, featured a symmetrical balancing of proportion, forms, and details in buildings.

   Women's education in the eighteenth century was uneven. Wealthy females learned reading, writing, arithmetic, and occasionally French. Most girls were restricted to learning only rudimentary book skills. All girls learned to sew, cook, and manage households.

   As white American males declared independence in 1776, large numbers of **enslaved Americans** lacked the freedom to choose their place of residence, vocation, and way of life.

   American individualism is entwined with America's sense of itself. From the earliest days, settlers on the frontier sought opportunities to better their lot in life.

   The birth of American manufacturing in the eighteenth century helped break the country's dependence on imported British goods and led to the full-scale industrial revolution that occurred in the nineteenth century.

   Chinese export porcelain was popular among wealthy Americans during the eighteenth century.

   Ask the participants if they have any initial questions about the difference between a *topic* and a *theme*.

2. Turn each *topic* developed for your site into a *draft thematic sentence.* Choose one topic and, with the group, develop a rich and full sentence that turns it into a *theme*, much like the examples cited above. Write the final version below the topic on the flip-chart page. Ask if there are any questions.

3. Divide the participants into groups of two or three. Give each group some scratch paper and a flip-chart page (or pages) from Activity 2.3. Ask each group to turn all of the topics on their flip-chart page(s) into draft theme sentences, writing the final sentences on the flip-chart page under the corresponding topic. Give people about fifteen minutes to complete this task. When they have finished, ask each group to post their flip-chart pages so that everyone can see them.

4. Read each theme sentence out loud, asking that people refrain from comments or questions until all theme sentences have been heard.

5. Open a discussion. Encourage comments, observations, and questions such as:

   Are any of the thematic sentences so peripheral that they distract from the main stories of the site? If so, should they be eliminated? (Put a black "X" next to these sentences.)

   Which sentences seem to express the most important ideas at the site?

   Which sentences express similar ideas or suggest a single, overarching theme?

   Is there anything important that is missing?

6. Use colored markers to identify all the sentences that belong to or suggest a similar set of ideas or an "overarching subject." For example, for the Caleb Crawley House, all the sentences that related in some way to eighteenth-century patterns of work, education, and socialization might be marked in purple. All the sentences related to the Crawley family's patriotism might be marked in green. A number of the sentences are likely to fit under more than one overarching subject category. Mark these with all of the relevant colors.

   Ask everyone to look at the revised thematic sentences, most or all of which should now be linked into three to five larger subject groups. Encourage people to make any revisions or comments to improve or strengthen these overarching subjects and their supporting thematic sentences.

7. Ask a few of the participants to rewrite the sentences so that all those with one color, that is, in one "overarching subject group," are together on one or two flip-chart pages. Ask them to give each subject group a number (e.g., "overarching subject group #1") and a relevant identifying heading or title (e.g., "social life," "architecture," "politics," "women's education").

8. Ask everyone to look at the revised thematic sentences, which are now linked into larger idea/subject groups. Encourage people to make any revisions or comments to improve or strengthen these overarching subjects and their supporting thematic sentences.

9. Distribute Worksheet 2.3, *Outline: Using Sentences, Historical Context, Biographies, and Physical Evidence to Build Themes*. Reconvene the groups that met in step 3. Give each group one or two of the flip-chart pages that list an overarching subject and its supporting draft thematic sentences. Ask them to complete the worksheet, with the goal of creating a strong *theme* for each thematic grouping. The theme should incorporate the information in the group's draft thematic sentences, and reflect the strength of the physical evidence, biographies, and historical context at the site. Encourage them to refer to Reading 2.1 for examples. Give the groups about fifteen minutes to complete their worksheets.

10. Reconvene the participants. Ask each group to read their theme(s) aloud. Write each theme on a clean flip-chart page. Encourage discussion, comments, suggestions, and revisions for each theme.

11. Ask the group to review each of the themes. Ask them to begin to prioritize the themes, from most important to least. Do this through a discussion leading to a consensus. Some groups may prefer to vote to reach this decision. If so, give each person three colored dots and ask that they put a blue dot on the theme they think is most important, a red dot on their second choice, and a green dot on their third choice. Once everyone has voted, look at the various themes with their

collected dots and see if a pattern of preference is apparent (this generally happens). Using this evidence, work as a group to arrive at a prioritized list of themes.

12. Lead a wrap-up discussion. Aim for a consensus about the three to five themes identified for the site, their wording, and their overall ranking in importance. Encourage people to brainstorm about where these themes can be illustrated on the site (physical evidence) and how tours can begin to focus on these messages. Collect the worksheets for reference by staff who will be developing the thematic tour outline in chapter 3.

13. Thank everyone for their tremendous contributions to the site and its future interpretation to the public! Encourage the consultants to stay in touch if they have additional ideas that would contribute to the development of thematic tours for the site. Say that the site will similarly stay in touch, sending the new thematic tour outline that will be developed by the staff using the process outlined in chapter 3.

Outline: Using Sentences, Historical Context, Biographies, and Physical Evidence to Build Themes

Overarching Subject Group #1:

Ideas that support or are related to this subject (culled from the draft theme sentences):

1.

2.

3.

Evidence (cite several locations and/or specific objects on the site that illustrate this subject and its supporting topics):

1.

2.

3.

Biographical information (Which historical person or people can be used to discuss this theme and its supporting topics?):

Historical context (background information visitors need to know to understand this subject and its linked topics):

THEME:

Using the sentences and various historical evidence as a foundation, **write a strong *theme*** that conveys a significant message about the site.

Overarching Subject Group #2:

Ideas that support or are related to this subject (culled from the draft theme sentences):

1.

2.

3.

Evidence (cite several locations and/or specific objects on the site that illustrate this subject and its supporting topics):

1.

2.

3.

Biographical information (Which historical person or people can be used to discuss this theme and its supporting topics?):

Historical context (background information visitors need to know to understand the topic):

THEME:

Using the sentences and historical evidence as a foundation, **write a strong *theme*** that conveys a significant message about the site.

CHAPTER 3

Creating: *Writing, Revising, and Testing the Thematic Tour Outline*

THE ACTIVITIES CONDUCTED DURING THE ROUNDTABLE WORKSHOP will help the site refine the three to five interpretive themes and produce a new storyline that incorporates those themes. **The storyline and themes developed for the site will form the intellectual basis for the development of the thematic tour.**

Prior to beginning work on the thematic tour outline development process, it is important to review and revise the draft themes. To do this,

- Circulate the three to five themes developed during roundtable workshop Activity 2.4: *Identifying the Site's Themes* to the staff members who participated in the roundtable workshop; request comments and reflections.
- Along with the draft themes, circulate some questions to guide the staff in their thinking about the themes. The questions might include:

  Do the themes express the three to five most important ideas you want visitors to learn at the site?

  Has something important been left out?

  Are the themes expressed coherently and succinctly?

  Can these themes be easily incorporated into an interpretation that is lively and engaging?

  Are the themes easily illustrated by the physical evidence and historical biographies at the site?

  Do the themes encourage connections to contemporary life?
- Revise the themes as needed.

To create a thematic tour, staff should first develop a tour outline. The outline will ensure that all the key concepts are covered. It will also identify the array of physical evidence and the relevant historical biographies that can be used to convey the storyline. A tour outline also must be flexible so that guides can personalize their presentation and adapt it according to visitor needs and interests.

Staff should plan to spend a day working together to create a new thematic tour outline for the site. This outline should address two key components:

1. **Content:** the site's storyline, themes, physical evidence, historical biographies, and historical context and the interpretive stories that weave this information together.
2. **Logistics**: *where* people will hear particular content and *how* they will move through the site.

Creating a new thematic tour outline can occur in several ways. One approach is to have the project coordinator draft an initial thematic tour outline, then refine it with staff input. The other approach is for the staff to work together to create the thematic tour outline. A site should choose (or adapt) the strategy that best fits its particular needs.

Option 1: The Project Coordinator Creates a Draft Outline to Be Reviewed and Revised by the Site Staff

This process requires the project coordinator to follow these steps:

1. **Draft a storyline for the site**, using the cards developed in Activity 2.1 of the roundtable as reference. Incorporate the site's identified themes, appropriate physical evidence, biographies, and historical context. The storyline is the touchstone that encapsulates the most important messages the site should convey to the public. Circulate this draft to the staff for their comments. Make revisions as needed.
2. **Draft a thematic tour outline for the site**. To do this, identify each space that will be interpreted on the site. For each of these spaces, complete Site Staff Worksheet 3.1, *Drafting a Tour Outline,* found on p. 44, incorporating the ideas and materials developed during the roundtable workshop. Be certain to include a worksheet for all spaces where historical context, introductions, transitions, and a friendly farewell will be presented. Arrange the completed worksheets in a sequence that potentially could work as a guided tour. Prepare a summary cover sheet that lists each space in order. Photocopy the draft storyline, summary, and worksheets, making one set for each staff member. Circulate the document, saying it is a preliminary storyline and thematic tour outline for the site. Ask staff to review the material.
3. Schedule a staff meeting to discuss the draft storyline and thematic tour outline. Include all the staff members who participated in the roundtable.
4. Start the meeting with a discussion about the draft storyline. Ask staff for their comments and suggestions. Make notes and revisions as needed. If possible, reach a consensus and write the accepted new storyline on a clean flip-chart page. After the meeting, copy the storyline and circulate it to participants.
5. Turn to the proposed thematic tour outline. Ask for any general comments, noting especially suggestions for significant changes to the tour order or content. If there is a consensus about changing the tour sequence, rearrange the individual pages of Site Staff Worksheet 3.1, *Drafting a Tour Outline,* to reflect the new order.
6. Ask the staff to take the revised tour as proposed, moving through the site space by space in the sequence that has been identified. (An acceptable, but less desirable alternative is to take a "virtual tour" of the site, remaining in the meeting space and imagining each space that is to be interpreted.) As part of this sample tour, staff should review and discuss the main points or topics to be considered in each space, carefully linking the various forms of evidence with one or more of the themes chosen for the site.
7. Take notes, leading toward a revised outline that reflects this staff input.
8. After the sample tour, meet together to discuss the tour. Encourage questions, comments, ideas, and alternatives. Work gradually toward a consensus among the staff about a preferred tour route, the chief messages to be delivered at each stop along the way, and a suggested list of material culture and historical biographies that illustrate most strongly the themes being interpreted in each space.
9. Make a revised thematic tour outline that reflects this input. Circulate it among the staff for comment, then make revisions as needed. Create and distribute the **first draft** of the new **thematic tour outline**.
10. Implement Site Staff Activity 3.5, *Testing and Revising the Thematic Tour Outline.* Make revisions to the outline as needed. Circulate this new version to site staff and members of the theme development team. This is the **final draft** of the **thematic tour outline**. It will underpin the new thematic tours of the site.

Option 2: The Staff Creates a Thematic Tour Outline

This process requires the project coordinator to follow these steps:

1. Review Site Staff Activities 3.1–3.3 and be prepared to lead them.
2. Schedule a staff meeting (either one full day or two half days). Include the staff members who participated in the roundtable. If possible, choose a day when the site is closed to the public to facilitate working in the various site spaces. As preparation, ask staff to review their notes and worksheets from the roundtable workshop and the revised themes. Tell staff the goal of the meeting is to work together to create a new thematic tour outline for the site and the day will include time for discussion as well as more structured activities.
3. Prior to the meeting, make lots of photocopies of the Site Staff Worksheet 3.1, *Drafting a Tour Outline*. Each staff member will need one for reference. In addition, ask one staff member to keep a master set of the worksheets, which will include one completed worksheet for each interpreted space on the property.
4. Prior to the staff meeting, decide whether to conduct the activities by walking through the property (the real tour) or by remaining in the meeting space (the "virtual tour"). The real tour is preferable but may be difficult if the site is open to the public. Make any necessary preparations to assure that the chosen strategy works well.
5. Lead the staff meeting. State that the goal is to work together to write a new storyline for the site and create a thematic tour outline. Encourage a brief discussion about the ideas and materials generated during the roundtable workshop. Take notes.
6. Facilitate Site Staff Activity 3.1, *Revising the Storyline for the Site.*
7. Facilitate Site Staff Activity 3.2, *Building the Thematic Tour Outline*. Upon completion of this activity, take a break or end for the day.
8. Facilitate Site Staff Activity 3.3, *Testing the Thematic Tour Outline*. At the completion of this activity, take a break.
9. Facilitate Site Staff Activity 3.4, *Refining the Thematic Tour Outline.*
10. Upon completion of the four activities, lead a wrap-up discussion to encourage an enthusiastic consensus about the thematic tour outline that has been drafted.
11. After the staff meeting, use the materials assembled in the four activities and any notes generated by the discussions to produce a refined thematic tour outline for the site.
12. Circulate this outline to staff for comment. Make any revisions that are appropriate. Create and distribute the **first draft** of the **thematic tour outline**.
13. Facilitate Site Staff Activity 3.5, *Testing and Revising the Thematic Tour Outline.*
14. Make changes to the thematic tour outline as needed. Create and distribute the **final draft** of the **thematic tour outline.** This is the document that will underpin new thematic tours of the site.

Revising the Storyline for the Site

Purpose: To draft a new storyline for the site.

Time: Thirty minutes

Preparation: Assemble materials
- 3 × 5 cards developed in Activity 2.1 of the roundtable workshop
- Blank 3 × 5 cards
- Easel, flip chart, and markers
- Copies of the revised themes

Procedure:

1. Read aloud the index cards developed during Activity 2.1 of the roundtable.
2. Ask everyone to close their eyes and take a "virtual tour" of the site. Encourage staff to walk through the site mentally, noting particular places or spaces that convey powerful impressions and messages. Open a brief discussion based on this experience.
3. Distribute new 3 × 5 cards and copies of the revised themes to each participant. With the memory of the rough draft storylines, the themes, and the virtual tour in mind, ask each person to revisit and answer the question "*[this historic site] tells the story of. . . .*"

   ❖ *This activity can also be done as a brainstorming session, with notes taken on a flip chart if staff prefers.*
4. Open a discussion. Keep it brief and fast-paced. Encourage people to read their cards, making notes on the flip chart. Pepper the discussion with questions, if needed:

   What is the story of the site?

   What key physical evidence makes this site special, therefore adding weight to the site's story?

   What key historical figures add life to the story?

   Have we forgotten something important?

   Is this story interesting to the general public? If not, within the limits of the site and its documented history, how can we make this story more interesting, compelling, and memorable?
5. Move toward a consensus. Encourage people to brainstorm to draft the new storyline. Write this on a flip chart. Take this version and say that you will polish it and distribute it to the staff for comment and final approval within the next few days.

Building the Thematic Tour Outline

Purpose: To develop a preliminary interpretation of individual spaces and develop a rough tour outline for the site.

Time: About two hours

Preparation: Assemble materials

Flip chart, easel, and markers
Photocopies of revised themes
Site time line, historical biographies, storyline, etc., as desired
Photocopies of the site floor plan and landscape plan; if possible, have an enlarged version to post at the front of the meeting room
Reading 3.1, *Storylines, Themes, Physical Evidence, Biographies, and Historical Context: Pulling It All Together*
Site Staff Worksheet 3.1, *Drafting a Tour Outline*
Post-it® notes
A big table

Procedure:

1. Distribute Reading 3.1, *Storylines, Themes, Physical Evidence, Biographies, and Historical Context: Pulling It All Together.* Give everyone a few minutes to read and ask if there are any questions or comments.
2. Distribute copies of the revised themes. Give everyone a few minutes to read and refresh their memories about the ideas and themes developed during the roundtable workshop.
3. Distribute and ask staff to skim Site Staff Worksheet 3.1, *Drafting a Tour Outline.* Distribute photocopies of the site's floor plan (and/or its landscape plan if the site places a heavy emphasis on outdoor interpretation).
4. Using the plan(s) and the various resources, lead a discussion by asking the staff to list all the possible interpretive spaces on the site. Write these on a flip chart.
5. Tell staff that it is time to make decisions about a thematic tour outline, using both this list and Site Staff Worksheet 3.1, *Drafting a Tour Outline.*
6. As a group, either go to the site or agree to stay in the meeting room to take a "virtual tour." (There are advantages and disadvantages to each. Choose the option that best suits the overall needs of the planning process.)
7. Using the list developed above, address each interpretive location using Site Staff Worksheet 3.1, *Drafting a Tour Outline,* as a guide to identify and discuss the appropriate *themes, context, biographies,* and *physical evidence.* Encourage everyone to include a variety of historical characters (owners, children, servants, laborers, etc.) as part of this discussion. Spur the staff to think carefully about the *main* point or message that should be interpreted in each space. Ask one person to serve as the scribe, completing one worksheet per location. (These will be rough drafts and should reflect the consensus view reached after some discussion.)
8. Once worksheets for each identified space are complete, ask if there are other spaces that should be considered. If so, add these to the flip-chart list, then examine those spaces and complete a

worksheet. By now, there should be a substantial number of completed worksheets for each of the spaces on the property that potentially can be interpreted to the public.

9. If this work was done by moving through the site, return to the meeting room.

10. Ask everyone as a group to spend a few minutes looking at the various flip-chart pages, worksheets, and floor plans, which should be spread out on the table. Ask how the different spaces cited on the individual worksheets could be arranged into a logical tour sequence moving through the site.

    Discuss and begin to make decisions as a group. To facilitate and visualize the process, mark the sequence on the floor plan, attaching Post-it notes with the sequence number on each interpreted space. For example, decide where the introduction should occur and stick a Post-it marked with a "1" on it. The next interpreted site would get a "2," and so on. Moving through the site, work toward a consensus about the sequence and the interpretive content of the tour. List this sequence on a clean flip-chart page. Now ask staff to look at these spaces and the interpretive information about them that appears on Site Staff Worksheet 3.1, *Drafting a Tour Outline.* Ask,

    With the current sequence, do the site's themes flow naturally or are they disjointed, confusing, or less effective than they might be? Should the sequence change to reflect these considerations?

    If necessary, make a new list reflecting this sequence on a flip-chart page.

    Now take the master set of worksheets completed for each interpreted space on the site. Spread them out on the table in the sequence cited on the flip-chart list. Ask,

    Will this order work? Will the tour flow both in its content and logistics? Will visitors feel comfortable and understand where they are going and what they are hearing? Are further adjustments needed?

    If so, make these adjustments on the flip-chart list and rearrange the worksheets on the table. Then ask,

    Using this route, what spaces on the site might work as transition spots—places to pause, shift gears, link themes, rest, answer questions, or offer interesting historical context that enhances but is not central to the presentation of the main spaces?

    Complete a separate worksheet for those transition spots that staff decides are important. (It is likely that there will be little thematic material in these transition spaces, but indicate on the worksheet the purpose of this space.)

    Now ask,

    Where should the tour welcome and introduction occur? Where should the wrap up and the farewell occur? What information must be included in the welcome and the farewell?

    If these spaces have not already been identified, complete a worksheet as needed.

    Discuss where these additional pages fit within the overall order identified for the main spaces of the site. Insert these new pages in their appropriate spots.

11. Number the pages sequentially—main spaces and minor—and state that for now this is the draft tour outline that the class will follow on a dry run.

Storylines, Themes, Physical Evidence, Biographies, and Historical Context: Pulling It All Together

Using the site's storyline as a foundation, thematic tours stress **themes**, amplified by **physical evidence, short biographies** and **historical context**. Two interpretive commentaries for the Caleb Crawley House illustrate how this combination can be used.

For example, a guide standing in the Crawley House parlor might say,

> The Crawleys entertained their guests in the parlor, offering them refreshments, which they served on this elegant tea table. At first, both men and women stayed together to talk and drink tea. After a bit, though, the men adjourned to Caleb's office, where they enjoyed sipping Madeira and other stronger beverages. Elizabeth remained here with her friends and poured tea until each woman indicated she had drunk enough by placing her spoon over her teacup. At that time, the ladies would adjourn and Rachel would take the used teacups to the kitchen, where she washed them.

This statement, amplified by physical evidence and biographical information, addresses the site's second theme: wealthy *Americans had distinctive patterns of work, education, and socialization.* When a guide delivers a good interpretive statement such as this, it engages a visitor for the moment, but also contributes to a cumulative message and memory that the visitor will take from the site.

As another example, a guide might interpret the garden at the Crawley House by saying,

> Elizabeth Crawley loved her garden. Some of her roses, or descendants of them, still grow here. Perhaps her most interesting horticultural activity, though, was her attempt to grow white mulberry trees. She, like Benjamin Franklin and others, was interested in developing an American silk industry. She imported silk worms from China, hoping they'd eat the mulberry leaves and produce silk threads that could be woven into cloth. The experiment was not very successful. Elizabeth got enough silk to make just one dress, which we will see when we get inside. Still, her idea about domestic manufacture influenced her sons, who later founded one of America's first steam-driven textile mills.

While speaking directly to Elizabeth's interest in horticulture, these comments offer a memorable story illustrating the site's third theme: *energetic individualism is a bedrock of American independence.* Mulberry trees, silk worms, and the promise of seeing Elizabeth's dress all contribute to helping a visitor learn about this significant theme at the site.

These two examples demonstrate how the right interpretive comments, presented at a visually engaging location, bring life and vitality to a site's major themes. If the storyline and themes are the grand ideas you want to convey, the particulars of historical events, the people involved, and the site's physical evidence are the essential and memorable nuts and bolts.

Drafting a Tour Outline

Space (room name, outbuilding, garden, etc.):

Theme(s) illustrated in this space:

Cite as many examples as needed, but ***emphasize*** *the most important information*

1.

2.

Significant topics, ideas, or stories that illustrate the theme and are associated with this space:

1.

2.

3.

Material culture evidence illustrating above:

Link these if possible

1.

2.

3.

4.

5.

People associated with the evidence/stories:

1.

2.

3.

4.

5.

Historical context:

List the context visitors need to know in order to understand the themes and stories

1.

2.

3.

Testing the Thematic Tour Outline

Purpose: To test the thematic tour outline created in Site Staff Activity 3.2 by using it to take a tour of the site.

Time: One to two hours, depending on the size of the site and level of discussion

Preparation: Assemble materials

Photocopies of the sets of the worksheets completed in Site Staff Activity 3.2, arranged in the numbered sequence devised by the staff, one set per person

Post-it® notes

Procedure:

1. Distribute the worksheet sets and give everyone a few minutes to skim through them. Ask the staff to be prepared to give a short interpretation of each space. To make it easier, consider assigning specific spaces to each person.

2. As a group, go to the site and take a sample tour using the route agreed upon by the group in the preceding activity. Assure staff that this is not intended to be a perfect final tour. It is simply an informal dry run to test the tour sequence and tour content. (The project coordinator should carry the completed worksheets for reference and take notes as needed.)

3. Move to the space identified as the first location. Ask the assigned person to give a brief, impromptu welcome and introduction. Ask whether this space works well for this message. If yes, move to the next space. If no, consider alternatives, and if there is a consensus, move to a site that seems better for this message. Ultimately, the goal is to find the best space to start the tour, knowing that there will be times when tours will necessarily begin at other locations. When everyone agrees on this first location, move to the next interpreted space as noted in the draft tour outline.

4. At this next location, ask the assigned person to give a brief interpretation based on the ideas developed by the group and recorded on the *Drafting a Tour Outline* worksheet. Again, be attentive to whether the sequence works and whether revisions to the content are appropriate. Make notations on the worksheets to indicate these changes.

5. Follow this procedure through the site, moving from interpreted space to interpreted space in the sequence devised in Site Staff Activity 3.2. Be sure to include the transition spots and their necessary directions or background information. Take turns giving brief interpretations using the ideas that have been developed. Upon completion of the sample tour, return to the meeting space.

6. Ask everyone to spend a few moments to jot down thoughts about the tour. Encourage staff to consider a range of questions, including:

   What was good about this tour?

   What was less successful?

   What might be repetitive?

   What got left out (information, location, etc.)?

   What messages or location ended up being most memorable?

   Which ideas, themes, and objects were particularly compelling?

   Were the different perspectives of different historic characters considered as the tour moved through the property? In other words, was care taken to interpret how a variety of people used, lived in, or thought about these spaces?

Are sensitive issues raised that will require special attention during the development and implementation of the new thematic tour? How will this be done?

Did the tour work logistically?

Did the movement through the property flow in a natural way or did the route run into difficulties—a bumpy path that some might find difficult to traverse, backtracking, ending in a weak spot that made a weak point?

Was the tour too long? Too short?

What improvements might be made?

7. Open a brief discussion to consider these questions and the individual responses to them. If the group agrees to make changes to the thematic tour outline, alter the order of the worksheets as needed. If some ideas and suggestions seem less obvious, say that they will be revisited in the next activity.

8. Now, take the completed worksheets from Site Staff Activity 3.2, *Drafting a Tour Outline,* and rearrange them into the sequence that reflects the consensus of the staff. Write this revised sequence on a clean flip-chart page and indicate it with Post-it notes on the floor and/or landscape plan(s) of the site. This is the rough draft *thematic tour outline* for the site.

❖ *This outline represents the core material and ideas that will be part of the general tour of the site. Additional thematic tours that explore different ideas can be developed later, but it is crucial to get the core material in place first.*

Refining the Thematic Tour Outline

Purpose: To refine the thematic tour outline into a final draft that will provide the underpinning for new pilot tours of the site.

Time: Two hours

Preparation: Assemble materials

- Flip chart, easel, and markers
- Materials developed in Site Staff Activities 3.2 and 3.3:
  - Original set of worksheets, *Drafting a Tour Outline,* arranged on the big table in the order reflected in the rough draft tour outline
  - The flip-chart list, posted, which shows the site's spaces arranged in a rough tour outline
  - The floor and/or landscape plan with Post-it® notes indicating the rough draft tour sequence

---

Procedure:

1. Post the flip-chart page citing the rough tour outline. Also post the floor and landscape plan of the site. Arrange the completed worksheets, *Drafting a Tour Outline,* in the proposed sequence on a big table. Have everyone quickly review this material.

2. Open a discussion of the proposed tour outline. Use the flip chart to record important ideas or issues that need to be addressed or changes that should be made. Consider these questions:

   Were all the site's themes adequately addressed during the tour?

   Was there a balance—was one theme stressed too much or too little?

   Were the choices of evidence effective in communicating the themes?

   Did the tour route work well?

   Was the tour the right length, which for most sites will be about forty-five minutes to an hour? Was it too long? Too short? Was too much time spent in one space? Too little time in one space? Was the time spent in individual spaces appropriate within the context of the overall interpretation of the site?

   If the tour was too long, what should be cut? If the tour was too short, what could be added that would enhance the thematic interpretation of the site or be of general interest to visitors?

   Note these comments on a flip chart. Make any necessary changes on the worksheets and rearrange them on the table to reflect this discussion.

3. Ask staff to close their eyes and imagine walking through the site, space by space. Ask questions such as,

   Are there visually compelling spaces that are not addressed in the current tour outline?

   Is there an archaeological site that is temporarily open and highly visible; are there places in the farmscape where animals might appear (not on cue!) or where there are pungent smells?

   Is there a special exhibit of clothing in a bedroom?

   What changes should or could be made to include these "affective" experiences for visitors?

   Note these comments on a flip chart. If necessary, make new worksheets to reflect these additional stops on the tour.

   Remember: Keep a record of any suggestions about modifications to the furnishing plan that potentially could enhance the interpretive impact of the tour.

4. Think for a minute about the *non-thematic* pieces of the tour. Does the current rough tour outline offer the best answers to some important questions?

   Where will the welcome and introduction take place? What should be said?

   What transitions are needed to move from one main space to another? Where will these occur? What should be said?

   Where will the tour end? How will the interpreter close the tour to assure that people are left with a rich memory of their visit?

   Record these comments on the flip chart. Move the master set of Site Staff Worksheet 3.1, *Drafting a Tour Outline,* into the sequence that reflects these comments.

5. Ask staff to think about the three to five themes adopted for the site. Ask questions and note comments on the flip chart.

   Have any important ideas been added that don't quite fit the site's themes as they currently are written?

   Are some ideas becoming less important as the thematic tour outline emerges?

   Are there important or potentially interesting stories that are not on our tour outline because they do not directly support the site's themes? Should any of these stories be added to our thematic tour? If so, how can this happen in a way that enhances and does not distract from the thematic tour? Should the site consider developing a special subject tour around these unusual and perhaps idiosyncratic stories?

   Make changes to the themes or to the worksheets, if necessary. Make a list of special subject tours the site should consider developing.

6. Ask staff to look at the set of worksheets, arranged on the table in the sequence that reflects the tour outline. What additional changes or rearrangements should be made to reflect the discussion above? Discuss, then make changes as needed.

7. Ask staff if they agree that this new sequence represents the recommended thematic tour outline for the site. (By now it should. If not, make changes or continue to discuss until a consensus is reached.)

8. Ask the staff whether any changes should be made to the site storyline to strengthen its message and linkage with the new thematic tour outline. Discuss and take notes if revisions are suggested. Say that a revised storyline will be circulated for comment and approval.

9. Thank everyone for their help and input. Conclude the staff meeting by saying that the project coordinator will compile a polished thematic tour outline that reflects the day's activities and discussion.

   - Using the completed set of worksheets and their sequence, the project coordinator can compile a final draft of the thematic tour outline. Prepare a summary cover sheet that lists the site spaces in the recommended tour sequence.
   - The project coordinator should photocopy and distribute the summary sheet and sets of the worksheets, arranged in the sequence that reflects the new tour, to all staff and members of the theme development team. This set of worksheets will become the basis of the new **thematic tour outline.** Ask the staff and the theme development team to review the summary and worksheets and submit their comments. Make revisions as needed, leading to final approval by the staff and the planning team. Upon approval of the summary and worksheets, the project coordinator should work with other staff members to develop a tour outline that will be tested and revised as part of Site Staff Activity 3.5.

Testing and Revising the Thematic Tour Outline

Once the site staff has drafted a thematic tour outline, it is crucial to test the outline then revise it based on actual experiences with different types of audiences. Members of the theme development team can accomplish this by becoming temporary guides, using the outline as the framework for tours given to selected groups of visitors, staff, guides, or board members. This testing process necessarily must be more flexible than the more structured approach used in Site Staff Activities 3.1–3.4. Consider using or adapting this procedure:

1. Select four to six staff, guides, or members of the theme development team to give pilot tours. Divide the group into pairs and ask each pair to practice giving tours based on the new outline to one another. Encourage the teams to practice until each person feels confident and comfortable with the outline and can pilot the tour with "outsiders."

   ❖ *Remind "guides" that the tour outline is not a script. It is to be used as a skeleton on which their personal tours should be built.*

> By having current members of the guiding staff participate in the process of creating and revising the thematic tour, the site will pave the way toward helping *all* guides adopt it. Guides who have invested in this experience will be essential ambassadors of change. They also will be equipped to be *mentors* to new guides, both formally and informally. (See part 3, p. 135.)

2. Create a variety of tour groups composed of staff, guides, board members, and if possible, staff members from other nearby museums or historic sites. Schedule tours for them, led by a staff member who has devised a pilot tour. If possible, have another member of the thematic tour team observe the group. After the tour, encourage questions or comments by the participants. Then, the tour leader and the observer should meet and prepare a few written notes about their experiences, their observations of the audience, and the effectiveness of the outline.
3. At announced times, substitute the new thematic tour for the old general public tour. Again, it would be helpful for a member of the thematic tour team to trail the group as a quiet observer. Shortly after the tour, the guide and the observer should meet and write down their observations about their experiences, the effectiveness of the outline, and general impressions about how the visitors responded (Did they ask questions? Did they pay attention? Did they appear to be learning about the site and its themes? Did they appear to be enjoying themselves?).
4. Conduct enough pilot tours to determine the strengths and weaknesses of the new thematic tour outline. Compile and review all comments, then revise and edit the tour as needed. Prepare a new draft of the thematic tour outline that will be the working document used to train guides in part 2.
5. Consider, then choose, the most suitable tool(s) to evaluate the success of the thematic tours that the tour teams have developed. The most formal and sophisticated approach is to hire a professional skilled in audience surveys. This professional can perform the entire evaluation process, which can include such options as focus groups, questionnaires, and visitor surveys. A professional may also develop special tools that the site staff can administer, such as questionnaires. If hiring a professional is not an option, site staff will need to identify an evaluation strategy that it can administer. One useful option can be an informal survey of visitors after they have completed a tour or a visitor's comment sheet.

There is a considerable literature that discusses evaluation strategies for museum programs. Consult one or more of the references cited in the bibliography to help craft a good evaluative strategy suited to the site's needs. See, for example, Judy Diamond, *Practical Evaluation Guide: Tools for Museums and Other Informal Educational Settings* (Walnut Creek, Calif.: AltaMira, 1999).

6. Continue to monitor and evaluate the new thematic tours, even after the site guides have been trained, to assure regular improvement to its content and overall presentation. Make revisions to the thematic tour outline as needed and on a regular basis.

SAMPLE MATERIALS

3.1: TIME LINE FOR THE CALEB CRAWLEY HOUSE, 1763–81

3.2: SHORT BIOGRAPHIES FOR THE CALEB CRAWLEY HOUSE

Time Line for the Caleb Crawley House, 1763–81

Date	*Crawley House*	*United States*	*World*
1763	Caleb Crawley buys 400 acres of land for new country estate; hires farmer to begin cultivation	Seven Years War (French and Indian War) ends	French cede territory east of Mississippi and in Canada to British
1764	Construction of house and outbuildings begins; takes four years to complete		"Spinning jenny" developed in England, spurs textile manufacturing
1765	Caleb and Elizabeth Crawley have fourth and last child, Sarah (older brothers Benjamin and William, sister Anne)	Stamp Act imposed on colonies; rebellion and demands for repeal	
1766	Crawleys move into house, though it is still unfinished		
1767	Elizabeth Crawley plans garden; household includes Elizabeth and Caleb, four children, enslaved cook Rachel, indentured servants Lydie and Molly, manservant Horace, tenant farmers Robert and Jacob, various day laborers	Very unpopular Townshend Acts and import taxes imposed by parliament on colonies	
1768	Crawleys commission portraits and parlor furniture, still in house today		
1769	Caleb elected to provincial council; fire damages kitchen; quick thinking by Rachel prevents house from burning; Benjamin begins reading law with Joseph Galloway		James Watt patents steam engine, which later helps spark industrial revolution
1770	Crawleys purchase large table for second parlor, early example of dining room table, still in house today		
1771	Elizabeth keeps journal for one year, then stops; describes daily routines and records receipts (recipes)		

Date	Crawley House	United States	World
1772	Caleb meets with others opposed to British colonial policies; warned by royal governor about his "traitorous" activities		
1773	Sarah works a sampler, still in the house today; Rachel purchases freedom; Caleb arrested by order of royal governor for leadership in tea boycott	Boston Tea Party	
1774	Benjamin works as scribe for Continental Congress; supports nonimportation agreements that force merchants to cease trade with England	First Continental Congress called to Philadelphia	Louis XVI ascends French throne
1775	Caleb a member of provincial council that raises militia to oppose British troops	Revolution begins; Lexington and Concord; Second Continental Congress	
1776	Caleb corresponds with Continental Congress delegates. Reads *Common Sense*, his copy of which is still in house	Declaration of Independence	
1777	Caleb joins Continental Army. Elizabeth cares for children, runs household, manages farm with assistance from her sons; she keeps journal for remainder of war	American win at Saratogas spurs alliance with French against British	
1778	Caleb at Valley Forge	British leave Philadelphia	
1779	Benjamin joins Continental Army. Letters between Elizabeth, Benjamin		English invent spinning mule; it revolutionizes manufacture of spun thread, of spun thread, paves way for textile industry
1780	Caleb in New York, writes home about treason of Benedict Arnold		
1781	Benjamin and Caleb with Americans in Virginia. Letters home. They return home in December	Cornwallis surrenders to Washington at Yorktown	

Short Biographies for the Caleb Crawley House

❖ *These fictional "biographies" are samples intended to illustrate the type of information sites should include when they develop their own historical biographies. Sites may need to conduct new research to be able to prepare some of them (e.g., for servants or slaves). In some cases, where research is not possible or information is unavailable, it will be necessary for sites to develop representative biographies using information culled from published materials. The goal of these short biographies is to bring historical people to life in ways that have meaning for guides. Guides, in turn, will incorporate these "people stories" into their tours, bringing the site to life for visitors.*

CALEB CRAWLEY (1730–1801)

Caleb Crawley was the eldest son of William and Anne Haines Crawley. He was born in Burlington, New Jersey, and lived in that area most of his life. Raised a Quaker, he attended Quaker schools prior to training as a lawyer with William Allen in Philadelphia. By the mid-1750s he had a thriving law practice in Burlington. His support of the French and Indian War (1754–63), which required colonies to raise militias, led him to leave the pacifist Society of Friends. His law practice flourished and by 1763 he had joined other wealthy colonial Americans in a postwar building boom that resulted in a wave of new country houses and urban mansions. That year Caleb purchased four hundred acres near Burlington and immediately began plans for a country house and farm. From this location he could be both a lawyer in Burlington and a gentleman farmer. He built an elegant brick house patterned on plate 1 of the English architecture book, *Designs in Architecture,* by Abraham Swan. Local craftsmen, led by master carpenter Thomas Thompson, spent four years constructing the mansion, its barn, several outbuildings, and a small pavilion that overlooked a fish pond. It was the finest country house in the area.

Caleb first sought public office in 1765, when he vocally supported overthrowing the hated Stamp Tax imposed by Parliament. He lost, but two years later was elected to the provincial council. It was within this setting that he developed strong connections with radicals who supported independence of the American colonies from Britain. By 1773, he was an ardent patriot at a time when many of his neighbors considered the Boston Tea Party an overzealous response to the tea tax. These radical beliefs and actions led the royal governor to have him arrested for treason. After his release in 1774, Caleb urged the provincial council to raise a militia. He read *Common Sense* by Thomas Paine in 1776, and his signed copy remains in the house. He corresponded with members of the Continental Congress meeting in Philadelphia and his letters offer a personal window on the events leading to the adoption of the Declaration of Independence. He joined the Continental Army as a major in 1777 and was in regiments that engaged in many of the significant campaigns of the Revolution. Again, letters home describe his experiences, with descriptions of events ranging from the dire straits of Valley Forge to the jubilation of Washington's ultimate triumph at Yorktown.

After the war, Caleb retired to his farm. He experimented with new agricultural techniques and encouraged his sons to develop domestic manufactures so the new United States would not be overly reliant on England. He corresponded with Revolutionary leaders and enjoyed telling his grandchildren about his life. Caleb's remarkable experiences in helping create a new nation instilled intense pride in his descendants. They maintained the Crawley House and its contents in tribute, until the last direct descendant, Elizabeth Crawley Stewart, gave the house and its collections to the new Crawley House Foundation in 1976.

ELIZABETH BUDD CRAWLEY (1734–1816)

Elizabeth Budd, the daughter of Hannah and Benjamin Budd, was born in Mt. Holly, New Jersey, in 1734. She and her family were members of the Society of Friends, which encouraged a good education for daughters as well as sons. Elizabeth attended a Quaker school in Mt. Holly, where she learned reading, writing, arithmetic, geography, simple bookkeeping, and sewing. While at school she stitched the exquisite silk sampler that still hangs in the Crawley House. In 1752 she married a young lawyer, Caleb Crawley. She and Caleb had four children who survived infancy: Benjamin (1754), Anne (1757), William (1760), and Sarah (1765). Elizabeth lost four infants in childbirth.

Elizabeth used her education throughout her life. She loved books and assembled a sizeable library, many volumes of which remain in the house. She particularly loved works on horticulture and botany. Her collection of English, American, and French treatises related to horticulture comprises one of the finest collections that survive from this period.

Elizabeth kept the household and farm accounts when Caleb was in prison and while he served in the Continental Army during the Revolutionary War. She wrote many letters to him, which survive because he saved them and brought them home. Also, she kept a detailed journal during the Revolutionary years that describes her everyday life during these tumultuous times. Her journal includes descriptions of slaughtering pigs, working with one son and her daughters to harvest the farm's wheat in 1778, remaking linen shifts three times because there was no fabric available for new ones, treating her daughter Sarah for whooping cough, and helping deliver a baby. She also wrote of the war. At times, she spoke of her loneliness and fear because her husband was in the army. She described the movements of both British and American troops through the countryside and the terror she felt in December 1776, when awakened by the muffled sound of cannons. Several days later she reported Washington's surprise victory at Trenton. Though as yet unpublished, her diary offers a vivid account of eighteenth-century life from a woman's perspective. This portrayal is enhanced by the rich detail about the Revolution and its impact on everyday Americans.

After the war, Elizabeth resumed the quiet life she had known. She stopped keeping her journal, instead devoting herself to creating a magnificent garden. Here she tested new plants, including mulberry trees, which she hoped would provide the basis for a new American silk industry. The project failed, but instilled in her sons a desire to pursue domestic manufactures. With their mother's support, they started a paper mill in 1785. Then, as an elderly woman, she had the joy of watching both sons start up a small but revolutionary textile mill that used imported English machinery to mass produce cotton fabrics for the American market.

BENJAMIN CRAWLEY (1754–1835)

Benjamin Crawley was the eldest son of Caleb and Elizabeth Budd Crawley. Until 1766 he lived with his parents, one brother, and two sisters in a brick house in Burlington, New Jersey. There he attended school, where he learned arithmetic, reading, writing, geography, natural history, Latin, some Greek, and astronomy. In 1766 his parents sent him to a boarding school in Philadelphia. He stayed there three years, then began reading law in the offices of Joseph Galloway, a leading attorney. During this period Benjamin was friendly with other young lawyers, who grew increasingly vocal in their denunciation of English policies in the colonies. His friendships led to a split with Galloway, a firm supporter of British interests. Benjamin left Galloway's office, practiced a little law, but mostly became more deeply involved with those who supported American freedom. This culminated in his serving as a scribe to the First Continental Congress, starting in 1774. There the twenty-year-old watched and recorded the heated arguments launched by steadfast Tories led by Galloway and radical patriots such as Charles Thomson. Benjamin's own political persuasions hardened and he became an ardent patriot, writing home about his fervent support of nonimportation agreements intended to cut economic ties with England. This profoundly shaped his interest in domestic manufactures, which for him furthered America's independence by breaking the country's economic dependence on England.

Benjamin returned home in late 1775 at the request of his parents. He helped his father with both his law practice and farm. He and his father read newspaper accounts of the increasing tensions between England and the colonies. They also read political tracts. His father's copy of *Common Sense* includes notes in the handwriting of both men. When his father joined the Continental Army in 1777, they agreed that Benjamin should stay home to help his mother with the farm and the family. Elizabeth reluctantly agreed in January 1779 to Benjamin joining the army, and he served until December 1781. He and his father were at Yorktown for Cornwallis's surrender, an event Benjamin recounted often for the rest of his life.

Upon his return to New Jersey, Benjamin at first threw his energies into making the Crawley farm one of the finest in the area. He tired of agriculture and returned to his dream of developing domestic manufactures. In 1785 he worked with his brother to build and run a paper mill. This venture was moderately successful and lasted until 1805. Then, at the age of 52, he took his biggest risk. He purchased new steam-powered machinery from England that was revolutionizing the production of textiles. With this English machinery, Benjamin started an American textile mill, one of the first in the country to rely on this new technology that ushered in the industrial revolution. The enterprise struggled at first, gained momentum during the War of 1812 and the embargoes on British goods, then settled into a pattern of steady growth and strong sales. As an old man, Benjamin loved telling his children and grandchildren that he beat the British on the battlefield, then beat them in the marketplace.

RACHEL JONES (C. 1750–1824)

Rachel Jones was born a slave. She was the daughter of Priscilla, owned by Elijah Smith of Salem, New Jersey. Priscilla served as a cook to the Smith family and likely trained Rachel in those skills. When Rachel was about fifteen, Smith hired her out to Caleb and Elizabeth Crawley. This was a relatively common way for owners to hone the skills of their slaves. Smith received a portion of Rachel's wages. She, however, kept a small portion, which she saved with the intention of purchasing her freedom. The Crawleys viewed this arrangement two ways. By hiring the enslaved Rachel, they acquired the services of a young, but well-trained cook. They also wanted to help Rachel in her quest for freedom and this arrangement was one of the best available at that time. Smith proved agreeable to letting Rachel stay with the Crawleys until she had saved the money she needed. In 1773, Rachel presented £50 to her former owner, Elijah Smith. She returned to the Crawley household and began earning full wages for her services. She also now was free to live and travel where she wished.

Rachel was an excellent cook based on descriptions of meals recorded in Elizabeth Crawley's letters and journals. Surviving receipts (recipes) suggest she had mastered the English style of cooking. They also indicate her familiarity with stews and soups that had distinctive Caribbean flavorings. This suggests that her mother may have trained as a cook in the Indies and come to New Jersey or Philadelphia as a young woman. That Rachel mastered and blended English and Caribbean cooking suggests her skill and creativity. Her recipes also offer evidence about the emerging American cuisine, which blended the techniques, recipes, and foodstuffs from a variety of cultures.

Rachel lived with the Crawleys in the room above the kitchen until 1795. Letters written by Elizabeth mention Rachel occasionally but one letter in particular describes how she saved the Crawley house. In 1769, a fast-moving fire in the kitchen nearly went out of control. Rather than run, Rachel coolly grabbed two fire buckets and started to put the fire out. Because there was not nearly enough water, she tore off her apron, followed by her heavy wool skirt, and threw them on the flames to extinguish them. Only then did she run out of the kitchen to shout for help, which brought more hands and more water to the cause. Though down to her petticoat, Rachel worked side by side with members of the Crawley family and together they put out the fire. The kitchen was damaged and required repair, but the fire did not spread and consume the house, which could easily have happened had Rachel not acted so effectively.

In 1795 Rachel left the Crawley household. She rented a small house in Burlington that still stands. There she lived until her death in 1824. She never married, but continued to work occasionally as a cook, even returning to the Crawley house to help with special events such as weddings. Mostly, however, she became known as a preacher. She took the last name of Jones in honor of Absalom Jones, the founder of the African Methodist Episcopal Church, which she joined and in which she became a leader. Her obituary noted that she was born a slave, bought her freedom, then became a leader in a new *American* church.

PART TWO

TRAINING GUIDES TO GIVE THEMATIC TOURS

Introduction

THE INTENSIVE PLANNING PROCESS REQUIRED TO DEVELOP thematic tours, outlined in part 1, will greatly aid the staff charged with training guides. Part 2 offers a course that will train guides to give thematic tours. Chapters 4–7 cover particular topics: *Site Specifics and Historical Context, Material Culture, Interpretive Themes and the Thematic Tour*, and *Communication*. Each chapter contains a series of activities designed to teach a particular concept in a participatory, interactive style. The activities are arranged sequentially to reinforce ideas developed in previous sessions. The chapters, too, are arranged in an incremental style, one step leading to another, which helps build the information and skills required to give thematic tours. Part 3, chapter 8, *Managing Guides Effectively*, provides information about hiring, supporting, mentoring, and evaluating paid and volunteer guides.

Guide training at historic sites and house museums traditionally starts with a series of programs, lectures, readings, and workshops that convey a wealth of information about the site. Underpinning these essential activities is a general philosophy that mastery of facts and information matters, especially at a place with such a rich and fascinating history. This type of training encourages guides to take pride in the quantity and quality of information they have acquired. This is a good thing. The trap, though, is that it can encourage guides to eagerly share *all* they have learned with visitors. This can be a bad thing. The fact is, while some visitors love hearing "everything!" many actively hate it, and most simply tune out as more and more facts wash over their heads.

This book takes guide training to the next step. It is designed to train guides to *interpret* history by weaving facts, context, and the site's resources into fascinating, memorable, and effective stories that bring a historic site to life for a broad-based public. Far from being watered-down history, this approach actually organizes information in such a way that the site becomes an engaging, three-dimensional laboratory where people see, hear about, experience, and think about complex ideas. Mastery of every date and name matters less than the development of well-presented, powerful stories that illustrate a site to its best advantage. At the heart of this book is the philosophy that **thematic tours given by well-trained guides serve history *and* visitors well**.

The activities presented in part 2 form a curriculum that will train both new and experienced guides to give excellent, informed, memorable *thematic tours* of a historic site. Following the precise course outlined in this book takes a lot of time, however, perhaps more time than some sites have available to train guides. While the full course is strongly recommended, some sites may have neither the time nor the budget to accommodate the entire training course. If this is the case, trainers should familiarize themselves with all the activities presented, then choose those that best suit the needs of the site and its staff. Trainers must find the right blend of training sessions to help guides acquire the knowledge and confidence they need to be successful in their work with the public.

Therefore, as preparation for leading this course, the trainer will need to:

- **Review part 2 of this book**. Identify those activities that fit the needs of your site best. Read and practice the various activities as preparation for teaching them. **This will enable you to design the guide training curriculum that you and your trainees will follow.**
- **Establish a budget for the course**, including the cost of speakers and materials.
- **Create a schedule of activities and lectures**, making sure to avoid existing conflicts at the site, such as special events or periods of heavy visitation. Send it to trainees before the first session. Emphasize that it is crucial that they attend the full training program if they wish to be considered as a guide at your site. If retraining current guides, emphasize the importance of improving interpretation at the site, specifically by using the newly developed thematic tour.

- **Identify and schedule speakers** who can give presentations on the facts, the context, and the overall story of your site. Identify and schedule related activities, such as tours of other sites.
- **Create a loose-leaf notebook for each trainee**. Include all those materials developed for the thematic tour roundtable workshop. Trainees will also use the notebook to assemble materials handed out during the training course.
- **Develop a bibliography for the training course.** Create an on-site library with copies or photocopies of assigned readings and other materials. List places where additional reference materials are available (public library, historical society, college, etc.).
- **Identify several experienced guides who can serve as *mentors* for new trainees.** Ask each mentor to attend the first few sessions with their trainee to establish a strong, collaborative working relationship. Request that the mentor be available for questions and moral support during the remainder of the training, and that the mentor be available when the trainee begins to practice giving tours (see chapter 8, p. 135).

❖ *This curriculum is designed specifically to meet the training needs of new and experienced guides who must learn and then present the site's new thematic tour. For subsequent years, once all guides are familiar with the new tour and its presentation, we recommend a two-tiered training strategy. Use the full curriculum to train new guides and adapt some of the activities, as appropriate, to create refresher courses for the experienced guides.*

CHAPTER 4

Site Specifics and Historical Context

GUIDE TRAINING MUST START WITH THE CORE OF INFORMATION that makes your site special. This information includes **site specifics**: when the site was built, who lived and worked there, important events, and important dates. It also includes essential background information—**historical context**—that visitors must know in order to understand the site. This will include topics in pertinent social history, decorative arts, landscape studies, political history, and economic history. The combination of site specifics and historical context will give your trainees a foundation upon which they can build an interpretation of the site. So, guides must get the *site specifics* and important *historical context* under their belts. But as a trainer, be clear that this information alone does not make a good tour. Rather, ***site specifics* and *historical context* are building blocks that start the process of creating strong thematic tours.**

❖ *The activities suggested in this chapter are fairly traditional, so they are not written as lesson plans, as will be found in chapters 5–7. Pick and choose those activities that work best for your site and its resources. Consider interspersing a few of these activities later in the training course. For example, schedule a special lecture or an intensive room study well into the training period as a way to add variety and interest to the learning process.*

GOALS

- Guides will learn the history of the site and master core information required for giving a tour. They will become familiar with the site's resources: archival and decorative arts collections, buildings, landscape, and staff.

- Guides will be presented with an overview of the historical context into which the specifics of the site can be placed.

TRAINING STRATEGY

- Extend a warm welcome to trainees to assure a positive training environment. From the beginning make people feel valued and appreciated. This will encourage people to do the hard work the site expects. It also encourages the spirit and attitude that the site must exhibit and share with its visiting public.

- Assign a mentor to each trainee. A mentor should be a veteran guide at the site who has participated in the development of the new thematic tour. She should be able to present this tour with knowledge and good personal style, eager to share her enthusiasm, and willing to spend the time required with the trainee.

- Motivate guides to learn about your site and its collections. This should not be hard. After all, learning about your site is probably one of the reasons why they wish to be guides. Certain of the suggested activities should be opened to experienced guides to enrich their knowledge. An in-depth session on a particular part of the collection, for example, will help sustain the interest of veterans. It will also open the opportunity for new guides and more experienced guides to get to know one another.

- Make sure context is front and center. People need to know the specifics about your site *and* they must be able to place it within the larger contexts of your region's history and American social, cultural, political, and economic history. You must decide which will work best at your site: learning its specifics or learning the larger context first. Regardless of sequence, you must work to interconnect the specifics with the context, stressing that this approach is the one you will expect as the guides develop their own tours of the site.

- Remember: there must be balance. A grasp of facts and information will enable a guide to respond knowledgeably to the needs and interests of visitors. Guides must know the site well, but tours must be more than a recitation of facts and identifications. Remind guides that facts, while important, are only *pieces* of the story they will learn to weave into their tours in succeeding training sessions.

TRAINING ACTIVITIES: A MENU OF OPTIONS TO USE THROUGHOUT THE TRAINING COURSE

Welcome and Introduction: Putting People *First*

1. At the first training session, make people feel *welcome.* If trainees feel welcome from the outset at the site, they are likely to extend that same *welcome* to the public when they give tours.

2. Invite all site staff to the first training session, and introduce them to the trainees. Explain the responsibilities and expertise of each staff member, and encourage trainees to seek them out when they have questions, suggestions, or other issues. Invite each trainee to say a few words about herself, including why she is interested in working with the public at your site.

3. Introduce those veteran guides who will serve as mentors to their trainees. Allow some time for them to get to know one another. Explain the role of the mentor: a site "pro" who is a friendly aide to help the trainee during the course and who will give skilled feedback during practice tours. Distribute the mentor/trainee agreement and checklists, ask the mentors and trainees to review them, and have the trainees put a signed copy in their training notebook (see chapter 8, p. 137).

4. Emphasize, from the beginning, that the site values its guides and their contributions. By making trainees feel valued from the outset, the site will encourage a positive training environment, which typically spills over into an enthusiastic embrace of the training program. As the trainer, state that you are available to answer questions and address concerns, beyond the training program. *Remember*: guides who feel appreciated for their knowledge and service will nearly always become excellent ambassadors to the public.

Readings

1. At the first training session, **distribute core information** about the site that interpreters can keep in their notebooks. These should include materials prepared for or developed by the roundtable workshop, such as:

   the mission statement
   site brochure
   site history (no more than five pages)
   a time line of significant events
   short biographies of the main historical characters
   a chart showing occupants or family relationships
   a bibliography of pertinent books and articles available on-site or at a nearby library
   a brief history of the area, if available

   Ask everyone to bring these notebooks to all training sessions, both for reference and to allow them to add materials that are distributed throughout the training course.

2. Throughout the entire training course, **assign readings from the bibliography** you have distributed. Start with readings that provide *essential* context for understanding your site. Later add readings that *enrich* this core. Plan to spend at least a few minutes discussing each assigned reading so that everyone understands its relevance to your site and the tours you expect guides to give. These discussions can take a variety of forms. With different readings and at different times, you might try:

   an open conversation about one reading, with chief points noted on a flip chart, or book reports presented by one person to the group, or
   having several people do related readings on one topic that can be discussed by the group as a whole.

   After each session, assign one person to write a brief summary of the reading or topic, which can then be reproduced for the guides' notebooks.

Lectures and Tours

CORE ACTIVITIES—PLAN ABOUT ONE HOUR PER LECTURE, TOUR, OR WORKSHOP

1. **Tour**—Require that all trainees take at least one guided tour of your site with a staff member or one of the site's best guides before they begin their own training. This will familiarize them with the site and its interpretation.

2. **Facts**—Ask fellow staff members and others to give lectures or workshops about the specifics of your site: its architectural history, the people who lived or worked there, its collections of material culture, its landscape, important events, etc. Schedule these lectures early in the training program to provide trainees with the essential core of information they must know and master.

3. **Context**—Identify those contextual topics that shape the story of your site. Samples include local history, architectural history, the Civil War, material culture, horticultural history, African American history, the Colonial Revival, immigration, and the life of children. For example, if your site has outbuildings and was once a working farm, schedule a lecture on local agricultural practices. Or, if your site has a strong collection of children's furnishings and toys, have someone speak on the history of childhood. Try to identify speakers who can address their topics knowledgeably, concisely, and with some flair. Then, schedule lectures, interspersing them throughout the training course. Films or documentaries can also provide an educational yet enjoyable way to provide historical background. Either create a list of interesting videos and suggest that people view them at their leisure or schedule a "screening time" when the class can watch then discuss the movie as a group.

   Be sure to start with topics that are key to understanding the significance of your site. This information will help trainees develop the thematic material addressed in chapter 6, *Interpretive Themes and the Thematic Tour.* But also sprinkle less central though interesting lectures throughout the course to maintain enthusiasm and interest. Invite experienced guides to these enrichment lectures to help establish good relations among the interpretive staff as a whole. **Conclude each lecture or special program with a discussion that links the information presented with themes pertinent to your site. Encourage guides to pinpoint specific ideas or facts that would make useful additions to tours of the site.**

   ❖ *It is likely you will have to pay speakers, so be sure to include these fees in your training budget.*

4. Conduct a **walking or driving tour of your site's neighborhood or community.** Place your site within its local context so guides will not think that it as an island separate from its community. As part of the tour, or as a follow-up discussion, identify buildings, landscapes, road patterns, or settlement patterns that have affected or are linked with the history of your site. Be sure to talk about change over time: what has been lost, what has been added, and what still survives.

Study Sessions—Learning the Site and its Collections

CORE ACTIVITIES—PLAN THIRTY TO SIXTY MINUTES PER ACTIVITY

1. **Do a "room study."** Choose a specific space at the site and go from object to object, architectural detail to architectural detail, or landscape feature to landscape feature. Identify each object or feature, emphasizing significant aspects or information. This approach requires a thorough familiarity with the collection and/or direct participation by the site curator or other resident specialist. After doing this, have the group look at the room itself and discuss its function and the historic people who would have used it. Encourage questions and discussion, but **remember, don't get too bogged down** with detail because trainees might get tempted to build a tour of little-known facts rather than an interpretive tour that tells a meaningful story.

2. If your site has **room books or room cards,** provide trainees with time to familiarize themselves with their format and content. Have them compare specific objects with their room book entries as part of learning

the site's collection. Having the trainees spend time with room books accomplishes two things: first, it helps people acquire concrete information and, second, and even more important, it gives them the confidence to know they can "rely on the book" if a visitor poses a technical question about an individual object. If your site does not yet have room books, develop a list of key objects in each exhibition space, including such basic information as date and place of manufacture, provenance, materials, and accession number.

3. **Tour archival and storage areas** so trainees become familiar with the site's resources and what's *not* on view. If your site has particularly strong archival material, consider assembling a group of manuscripts, photographs, pamphlets, maps, and other materials, and have the trainees examine them to build their understanding of the historic people and historic context that shaped your site.

4. Discuss **curatorial issues** at your site: current research, conservation projects, planned exhibits, and reinstallations. Also discuss **curatorial policies that affect them**: what can and cannot be touched and why, and where they can and cannot go under normal circumstances.

5. Hold an **open question session**. Have guides prepare questions about specific objects that perplex them, or which they find particularly interesting.

6. Distribute copies or transcriptions of several **primary source documents** (diary entries, letters, inventories, wills, or other materials) to help trainees learn something about the site in a "first person," experiential way. Choose documents linked with current research and that contribute to the overall understanding of the site's storyline and themes. Start by helping the trainees figure out what the document says (both literally, if the handwriting or wording is difficult, and more subjectively, in terms of how to interpret the information). Then, either with individual documents or with a small interrelated group of documents, ask questions about how primary sources deepen knowledge of the site and can be used to underpin its interpretation. Conclude by having trainees consider how this information might, or might not, be included in a tour.

ENRICHMENT ACTIVITIES—PLAN ABOUT ONE HOUR PER ACTIVITY

1. Ask the site's curator to conduct a connoisseurship workshop about one or more objects in the collection. For example, she might:

   "Take apart" a piece of furniture to show its construction; that is, open all the drawers and put them on the floor or a table for people to examine. Provide a flashlight so people can see the interior framing. If possible, pull the object out from the wall so people can walk around it and see the back. The emphasis of this exercise should be on learning how to use the eyes to discover information. Stress, though, that the level of detail gleaned from this type of examination is generally not appropriate for tours given to the average visitor.

   Fill a table with a group of objects (for example, ceramics). Discuss individual objects as a way to develop connoisseurship skills. The goal, again, is to train eyes and generally familiarize people with the site's collection. This will help people feel comfortable that they know the difference between Chinese export porcelain, Pennsylvania Dutch redware, English Staffordshire, art pottery, and Fiesta Ware.

   "Read" the architectural development of a building on the site. Stand in front of the building and have the group examine and identify its building materials. From there, ask them to focus on certain architectural details, such as window trim or the roof pitch, to see whether they offer evidence about the style or period of construction of the building. If possible, reinforce this visual information with photographs of buildings that are similar or photocopies of pattern book designs that may have influenced the building's design. Take the group around the entire building, asking them to read each facade. Ask whether there is a clear "front" to a building and how this can be determined. Ask whether there is a clear "back" of the building and how this can be discerned. How are these differences reflected in the interior of the building? Who would have used which side of the building? Ask the group if they see evidence of change to the building, whether it is an addition, an alteration, or a removal. If the building does have a structural evolution, help the group find the clues. For example, be prepared to show:

a clean seam in a masonry wall where an addition butts the original construction
a raised roof
a removed porch as evidenced by a scar
an enlarged window that is unlike the other windows on the building

2. Assign one **short research project** to each guide. The project could focus on an *object*, an *individual* connected to the site, or a particular *feature* such as the garden, an outbuilding, or the kitchen. It could also explore a *pertinent but more general topic*, such as eighteenth-century dining practices, servants at the site, nineteenth-century plumbing, or how the site came to be preserved in the twentieth century. Make sure there are resources available at the site to help with the research process. Encourage the class to visit other libraries, museums, or the Internet for additional information. Ask each guide to present her findings to the group at a future training session.
3. Encourage trainees to **tour nearby museums and historic sites** to see how others interpret their collections to the public. Schedule a time to swap notes on these visits, for comparing and contrasting emphases and methods, and to share overall impressions (see Activity 7.1 for a related activity).

CHAPTER 5

Material Culture: *The Physical Evidence*

MOST PEOPLE WHO WORK AT HISTORIC SITES LIKE BOTH HISTORY and objects. We tend to have stashes of books on favorite topics: the Civil War, American architecture, biographies, local history, travel guides to historic places. We also might collect old furniture, ceramics, postcards, toys, tools, or just plain "curiosities." It is this combined interest—liking to read about "old stuff" and liking to look at "old stuff"—that draws us to historic sites. We enjoy hearing about what happened there, especially when it offers the chance to see a *real* object: Thomas Edison's light bulb, the desk where the Declaration of Independence was signed, a worktable where women sat to mend clothing, a hand-wrought horseshoe, a pair of Native American moccasins. Such objects bring history to life because they capture our imaginations and suggest interesting stories. Plus they trigger an undeniable, almost child-like wonder: we catch our breath, shake our head, and in near disbelief murmur, "This is the *real* thing and it is two hundred (or two thousand) years old!"

Objects help us "see" the past and link us with humans who lived before us. This is the intellectual power and the emotional magic that **material culture** carries.

Historic sites are blessed with a wealth of material culture. The authentic resources that make up material culture, set in an evocative physical context, are what make historic sites unique. Material culture makes it possible to present history in a visually engaging, intellectually stimulating, and emotionally satisfying way. To take full advantage of this opportunity, guides must learn to "read" objects: individually, collectively, and within their context.

This chapter offers a training strategy to do that. It is adapted from work done by Barbara and Cary Carson. Using sequential steps this chapter will help guides to look at an object carefully, then ask a series of questions:

- **What is this object? (*identification*)**
- **What did it do? How was it used? (*function*)**
- **Who made it? Who used it? What meaning/importance did the object have for people in the past? (*people*)**
- **What are the relationships among the object, its functions, and the people associated with it? (*ideas*)**
- **What connections can we make between the story of this historical object and our own lives? (*interpretation*)**

An analytical and interpretive focus on material culture will help guides develop strong thematic tours.

GOALS

- Guides will learn that ***material culture* is the *physical evidence*** that both documents and illustrates the storyline and themes of a historic site.

- Guides will recognize how **a historic site's interpretation is derived directly from its material culture**. They will understand that material culture is an evocative, effective teaching tool that helps bring historic sites to life for visitors.

- Guides will understand that **material culture encompasses everything made or shaped by human beings**: buildings, objects (both two dimensional and three dimensional), and landscape features such as gardens, farms, and tree-lined drives.

- Guides will learn the technique of **"reading" material culture**, which is a key ingredient of a strong thematic tour.

TRAINER PREPARATION

- **Review the two readings in this chapter:** *Asking Questions of Material Culture* and *Interpreting Material Culture: A Five-Step Approach.*

- **Review the material culture at your site.** Think about how to use material culture as the physical evidence that illustrates the site's themes and its broader historical context.

- With the assistance of the curator, **identify ten to twenty objects** that clearly illustrate one or more of the site's main interpretive themes. (The number of objects will depend on how many of the activities you choose and on the size of the class.) Choose a variety of media, including landscape features and architecture, decorative arts, tools and implements, clothing, and photographic and archival collections. Go for rich, obvious examples that are fun to interpret. These will provide the basis for the training activities on material culture.

❖ *Curators are charged with the care of your collection. Ask for their help with the activities in the chapter and get their permission before moving any objects.*

TRAINING STRATEGY

- Inspire guides to seek a broad understanding of material culture. Be sure to stress that material culture includes "things": houses, tables, lamps, chairs, clothing, toys, tools, books, manuscripts, and maps. It also includes man-made features in the landscape: a garden, road, path, or the view of the garden or stable yard from the upstairs bedroom window.

- Emphasize that *interpretation* moves beyond the simple identification of individual objects and discusses how objects and groups of objects can be used to illustrate certain human experiences. Good interpretation links the objects and their related activities to particular themes presented at your site (Activities 5.1 and 5.2).

- Suggest ways guides can select particular examples of material culture to illustrate the storyline and themes of your site (Activity 5.3). Since historic sites typically have *lots* of material culture, guides must pick from a wide range of physical evidence as they build their interpretive tours of the site. The trick is to start on the right track and focus primarily on those examples that offer the strongest evidence of the themes and evoke the richest stories related to the storyline. While this may sound easy, it is often hard. Sometimes guides get sidetracked into describing an object they especially like, but which has minimal connection to the site's overall interpretive themes (the *My Favorite Things Tour*). Another ever-present trap is structuring a tour around the identification of one object after another (the *Pots and Pans Tour*). Both of these approaches undermine the value of a tour and leave visitors with little understanding of the site's importance or historical message.

ACTIVITY 5.1

Understanding Material Culture

Purpose: To introduce guides to the concept of material culture and the messages it holds for interpretation.

Time: Sixty minutes

Preparation: Assemble materials

One everyday object to analyze with the class: a box of Jell-O®, a chair, a credit card, a baseball cap, a road map, a computer disk, car keys, a TV remote, a plastic plate

Objects from people's pockets or purses for the class to analyze

Photocopies, Readings 5.1 and 5.2, *Interpreting Material Culture: A Five-Step Approach* and *Asking Questions of Material Culture*

Procedure:

1. Begin the session with an open discussion. Ask the class, *What is material culture?* If the class knows what it is, ask them to name examples of material culture, both generally and at the site. If they are not familiar with the term, give a quick accurate definition: *material culture is anything shaped by human hands.* Remind the class that material culture at a historic site is the evidence for the stories told to visitors. It is this evidence, the "real stuff" of history, that makes historic sites exciting and interesting.

2. Urge the class to come up with lots of examples of material culture. If necessary, ask some leading questions to make the list as wide-ranging as possible: *What about a house? A candlestick? A garden? A swing set? A Thanksgiving turkey? A computer? A highway?* Also, ask *What is NOT material culture?* Answers should include natural phenomena such as mountains, oceans, lakes, and wildlife. For fun, ask a few provocative questions: What about a zoo? A dam? A rose? A rose garden? The goal is to establish that *material culture* is anything that has been shaped by human hands.

3. Introduce the step-by-step analysis of material culture. Use one of the everyday objects, for example, the box of Jell-O, to demonstrate how to move sequentially through a series of questions. Hold the object up and ask the class:

   What is this object?

   How does it work? How is it used?

   Who made it? Who owns it? Who uses it? Who maintains it?

   What are the relationships between the object, its function, and the people associated with it?

   What does it say about our lives today?

4. Distribute Reading 5.1, *Interpreting Material Culture: A Five-Step Approach.* Give the participants a few minutes to read it.

5. Put people in pairs or small groups. Ask each group to choose one object from among their possessions. Ask each group to examine the object carefully using the *five-step approach.* When they have completed this task, reconvene the class and ask groups to present their objects and their findings.

6. Tell the class that a thorough analysis of material culture requires some knowledge about the historical context of the era when the object was made and used. This context—knowing the events and ideas of an era, how people thought and reacted, cultural attitudes and social practices—helps us understand the object and its importance. We carry our own period's context with us, but not the context of other places and times. The farther away the original period of the object is, the less context we are likely to have as part of our own world view. So, an older object often raises contextual questions we have to answer in order for its "message" to be understood.

7. Ask the participants to name some ideas or understandings that we implicitly share about the object analyzed in step 3. If this involves a box of Jell-O, for example, some context you might implicitly share would be:

   Jell-O is not a gourmet food

   Jell-O is frequently served in hospitals and other institutions

   Children often like Jell-O

   In the mid-twentieth century, Jell-O was a popular ingredient in molded salads and desserts

8. Tell the class that we can learn a lot from material culture, but that the information is often unfocused. A historic site should create a focus to structure the examination of its material culture, specifically by developing themes. A theme helps sites identify the type of information that will be most useful in interpreting the material culture as relevant evidence of an important story.

9. Using the object analyzed in step 3, create a theme or focus, and ask the class what they would want visitors to understand about the object, given that focus. Offer a different theme or focus, and repeat the exercise. If the class analyzes the box of Jell-O, for example, you might ask:

   If our theme revolved around the cooking practices and nutrition of mid-twentieth-century America, what would we say about the box of Jell-O?

   If our theme concerned the commercial and industrial practices of the mid-twentieth century, what would we say about the box of Jell-O?

10. Distribute Reading 5.2, *Asking Questions of Material Culture*. Ask the class to read it on their own prior to the next training session.

Interpreting Material Culture: A Five-Step Approach

Interpreters can maximize the interpretive information conveyed by an object by asking a carefully designed series of questions. This process involves examining an artifact thoroughly, then answering specific questions in sequence. The analysis, questions, and resulting information help transform an object from, say, a simple chair, to an example of *material culture*, that is, something shaped by human hands that speaks to aspects of the human condition. It is as *material culture* that objects become rich illustrations for important stories and ideas at historic sites. Interpreting *material* culture lies at the heart of a successful interpretive tour at a historic site. Here are steps that transform an object into material *culture* ripe for interpretation:

STEP 1. WHAT IS THIS OBJECT?

Identify the object: a stove, birdbath, chair, saw, toy. When was it made? What are its materials?

STEP 2. WHAT DOES THIS OBJECT DO? HOW WAS IT USED?

Examine the object and describe how it functioned. For example, consider a *chair*. Its intended use was seating. Look at it again; ask more questions. Is it plain or fancy? Was it part of a set? Could it have been used only in the room where it is now? Or would it fit—stylistically and functionally—in another place just as well? As another example, consider a *coal stove*. How did it work? How did it improve the heating or cooking technology of the house? Is it plain or fancy? Does this indicate where it might have been used?

STEP 3. WHO MADE THE OBJECT? WHO USED IT? WHAT MEANING/IMPORTANCE DID THE OBJECT HAVE FOR PEOPLE IN THE PAST?

Who made the *chair*? Who owned it? Who sat in it (owner, servant, child, male, female)? Who *didn't* sit in it? Who dusted it? What meaning/importance did the chair have for the owner? The maker? The maid? Who purchased the *coal stove*? Why? Who stoked it? Who was warmed by it? How important was the coal stove to the household: What role did it play?

STEP 4. WHAT ARE THE RELATIONSHIPS AMONG THE OBJECT, ITS FUNCTION, AND THE PEOPLE ASSOCIATED WITH IT?

Consider the *chair*. What was the relationship between its maker and its purchaser? What does this chair say about its owner's wealth, status, or way of life? How might the owner's contemporaries have viewed the chair: Was it similar to ones they owned? Was it old-fashioned? Expensive? Ordinary? What was the relationship between the people who sat in it and those who dusted it? In an interpretive tour, could the chair be used as a symbol of a particular person who lived in the house? How might its use, or status, have changed over time? Would it have been moved to another room? Would different people have used it when it got old?

Consider the *stove*. What is the relationship between the person who stoked it and the person it warmed? How does the stove represent improved technology? Compare its use with the open-hearth heating or cooking that it replaced.

STEP 5. WHAT CONNECTIONS CAN WE MAKE BETWEEN THE STORY OF THIS HISTORICAL OBJECT AND OUR OWN LIVES?

This question ties all the preceding information together, making an object a lively and accessible piece of history that will interest visitors. By moving from *identification*, to *function*, to *people*, to *historical themes*, and then to *connections with the present*, an object can be used as an evocative illustration of particular historical stories.

Go back to the chair, say a Chippendale chair located in a historic house parlor. By answering the preceding four questions you may have determined that it is made of imported mahogany, dates to about 1775, and likely came from a Philadelphia chair-making shop *(identification)*. Its obvious *function* was seating. But there were subtler functions too: it may have been part of a set and its stylishness may have helped convey its owner's status to visitors. It was handmade by an expert *craftsman*, and therefore was expensive when new. Its cost, fancy design, and placement in the parlor indicate it would have been used by the *owners* of the house *(people)*.

Pulling this information together establishes the framework for an effective interpretive story tied to the themes of the historic site. For example, the chair might help illustrate an interpretive description of the owner's socioeconomic status. Or maybe the site's themes mean the chair would be more effectively used as a way to discuss eighteenth-century entertainment or the interrelationship between different classes in the household. *The point is to employ the chair as a visual anchor for an interpretation that helps people understand a complex idea about the past.*

The final step in analyzing material culture and using it as an interpretive tool is to link it with contemporary examples and experiences. Compare the expensive, handmade, mahogany Chippendale chair with today's inexpensive mass-produced chairs that are sold worldwide. In this comparison, the rare eighteenth-century chair provides a lesson about the limited goods available *before* the industrial revolution. The modern chair illustrates the explosion of consumer goods made possible *by* the industrial revolution, something that continues to benefit most of us today.

Now go farther. The old chair, while originally intended for use, is today a museum object because of its beauty, craftsmanship, monetary value, and history—qualities that have evolved over time. Will the modern chair undergo a similar transformation? Why or why not? What might have been the equivalent of the mass-produced modern chair when the Chippendale chair was new? (A Windsor chair? A stool?) What might be the equivalent of a Chippendale chair today? (An expensive chair at a department store? A handmade chair at a craft show?) Had we lived two hundred years ago, what would *we* have sat in?

These kinds of questions will engage visitors to think about objects—in museums and in their own homes—as rich statements about human experiences. That is what it means to *interpret* material culture.

❖ *This summary is adapted from Barbara and Cary Carson, "Things Unspoken: Learning Social History from Artifacts." In Ordinary People and Everyday Life: Perspectives on the New Social History, ed. James B. Gardener and George Rollie Adams, 181–203. Nashville: Tenn.: American Association for State and Local History, 1983.*

Asking Questions of Material Culture

WHAT DO ARTIFACTS "SAY"?

All objects—large and small, new and old, plain and fancy—can yield rich information that contributes to our understanding of human experiences. Often people assume that history is only recorded in books or documents or other manuscripts that can be read. In fact, much history has never been recorded in this way, so to have a full understanding of the past it is important to "read" other evidence, whether archaeological remains, a house, or a chair. Strong interpretation results from an analysis of many different types of primary sources, as each can inform the other. Sometimes, though, this is not possible and it can be hard to understand the object that has lost its context or a document that mentions a coin we have never seen. What is exciting about historic sites is that they usually have many and even most of the ingredients that make for the most vivid history: documents of all sorts and physical evidence of all types. To take advantage of these resources it is essential to learn how to "read" artifacts, just as historians read a diary to discover information about the past.

Reading physical evidence—material culture artifacts—takes a little practice but it is quite easy once you have done it a few times. Start by looking at the object *closely*. Pose the questions a good journalist asks: *What* is it? *Who* made it and used it? *How* was it made? *Where* was it made? *When* was it made? Now you have some facts that can ground bigger, broader questions. Try these:

How can a house be a statement of its owners' or residents' interests, activities, and identities?
What does a garden reveal about the people who planted it and those who tended it?
What does this object say about daily work and daily routines two hundred years ago?
Does this object suggest anything about the people who typically did not leave much in the way of written records—children, servants, workers?
How does this object show the relationship of its owner or maker with the larger world of family, friends, community, nation, or the world?

Don't stop now. The questions only get more probing, interesting, and revealing. Try some like these:

How does this house compare with the homes of others located nearby?
Was the architecture of the house "trendy" or conservative? Was the house larger, smaller, or about the same size as its neighbors?
What technology did the construction of the house require?
Were gardens *de rigueur* or the result of one owner's interest in horticulture?

Now, move beyond specific objects for a moment and broaden the questions. Try some like these:

What is known about the people who lived and worked on this property?
Who were the workers—slaves, servants, governesses, gardeners, housekeepers, butlers, secretaries, farmhands?
Who were the tradesmen?
Who were the owners?
What were their daily lives like?
How did these groups interact? How did their lifestyles differ? How did their lifestyles compare with people of similar social or economic status who lived in other parts of the country?
How did the owners make the money required to maintain the property? Was their livelihood typical or was the owner an innovator? What opportunities did workers on the property have to break out of their class? How did these opportunities compare with those in other parts of the country?

Now come back to material culture and ask:

How can objects help answer these questions? How can material culture be used as an effective teaching device during interpretive tours of a historic site?

Now come back to material culture and ask:

How can objects help answer these questions? How can material culture be used as an effective teaching device during interpretive tours of a historic site?

Look around your site and identify the physical evidence—the two- and three-dimensional objects that support the answers you have found to the questions you have raised. Start to think of these objects as something more than *things* to be identified by name only. Consider them instead as material culture that offers physical illustration to historical events, ideas, and themes. Consider three examples.

A BRICK HOUSE

Architecture and building materials are highly visible physical evidence that convey important information about a site. Guides must know many facts about a site's buildings: the date of construction, the architect if there was one, the various craftsmen who laid bricks or did the carpentry, the style of the building, and the historical context or sources that influenced that style. This factual information, often uncovered during the research associated with a historic structure report, forms the basis for *interpreting* a building as a significant illustration of a site's themes and storyline.

To *interpret* a building it is useful to ask questions that start with the facts, using them to move in directions that suggest interesting and instructive ideas about the past. For example, how does a *brick house*, built in a small town in Ohio in 1819, illustrate information about the wealth and status of its original owner? How does it compare in style, size, and building materials with other houses built in the immediate area at the same time? How does it compare with houses built in other parts of the country at that time? Where did the materials come from to build the house and what does that suggest about transportation and communication routes? Who actually built the house? The owner? A carpenter? A team of specialized craftsmen? What does this information about the house, its materials, its owner, its craftsmen, and its relationship with buildings in the area suggest about life in Ohio in 1819?

Once the facts are established and the questions asked, guides at this 1819 brick house will be in a position to develop an interesting and memorable interpretation that weaves together physical evidence, good "people" stories, pertinent historical context, and linkage to the site's themes. A good interpretation may state that brick was used only on the town's most elaborate buildings in 1819, so its appearance here offers a good indication of the relative wealth and ambition of its original owner. The brick, too, offers a way to talk about a real danger in 1819: fire. The use of this fire retardant material may suggest the owner's desire to build as safe a house as possible for his family. Other building materials or details can contribute to this story, whether the expensive polished stone front steps or a sophisticated fanlight above the front door. A less elaborate rear facade may serve as a way to talk about how the owner spent more on the public side of the house and less on the side that would only be seen by the family and servants. The front of the house in fact may serve as a compelling backdrop to illustrate and interpret the public lives of the residents, while the rear may serve the same role for describing the private lives of the family and the servants.

With good facts, careful reading of the material culture evidence, provocative questions, and a well-developed interpretation, this brick house built in 1819 can become a focal point for presenting some of the site's most important ideas to the public.

> ***Historical message:*** *A building is a major piece of material culture evidence at a site. Its style, materials, usage, and comparisons with neighboring buildings can serve as powerful illustrations that convey information about the lives of the original residents and the time in which they lived.*

A CHINESE EXPORT TEACUP

By using a similar approach of combining visual evidence with good research, consider how a Chinese export teacup might be used to explore a variety of questions in a restored eighteenth-century Philadelphia house. For example, the teacup offers a good illustration of the economic status and social aspirations of its original owner. When new, say in 1750, the imported porcelain would have been expensive. Eighteenth-century Philadelphians would have recognized that. (To understand this, think about a contemporary situation. Today we know that bone china teacups are expensive, particularly in comparison with inexpensive earthenware coffee mugs.)

The exotic provenance of the teacup, too, might be used to describe the relatively sophisticated marketplace in eighteenth-century Philadelphia. Ships brought goods from thousands of miles away and merchants sold them to Philadelphians eager to enjoy new and lovely objects.

The teacup also can be used to describe a formal ceremony and social event, tea drinking, which was enormously popular in the eighteenth century but is unfamiliar to most people today. Finally, the teacup could be used to discuss class structure in eighteenth-century Philadelphia. Specifically, who got to drink out of the teacup and who did not? Who had to wash it and who did not? How would the rich tea drinker have viewed the teacup as opposed to a servant who drank from something quite different? When viewed from these multiple perspectives, the teacup, when new, said a lot about its owner: he/she was probably relatively wealthy and enjoyed having elegant objects as household possessions. The teacup also had a central role in a custom that illustrates eighteenth-century manners, class structure, social practices, and gender roles.

This same teacup, however, could be read quite differently if it were found in a house dating to (or interpreted to) 1875. By then it would be old, might be cracked, and conceivably could have lost its matching saucer. In this case the teacup, so elegant in 1750, might be interpreted as a "hand-me-down" suitable for use only by servants, children, or others of considerably less economic status than its original owner.

Finally, people today might recognize the same teacup as a valuable antique, desirable for its decorative appeal but probably never to be used to drink tea.

> ***Historical Message:*** Small objects can tell big stories about the past. An object may reveal information about styles that were popular, trading patterns, and social customs. The meaning or usage of an object may also change over time in interesting and important ways. When an old object is compared with modern examples, it helps visitors understand the past in personal ways.

A PORTRAIT

Now consider a portrait of a woman. Most likely, the sitter commissioned the painter to produce a canvas that would capture her image both for her own family and friends, and for posterity. The painting shows the color of her eyes and hair as well as the shape of her face. It might suggest her mood by the expression of her mouth. A large portrait will include details about her clothing—the fabric, the style, her accessories—that reveal information about her social status. Her setting—a chair or a landscape—may suggest something about her home or personal interests. When new, the portrait would have been an impressive object, that is, one that commanded the attention of visitors to the house. They may have said it resembled the sitter, or to themselves they may have muttered that it improved her looks. It might have carried special significance for certain people—a fond husband or children, who one day would inherit the picture and refer to it when talking about their mother to their own children.

Over time, though, the identity and the personality of the person in the portrait could easily be forgotten. It could become a dusty old picture of some unknown old lady in black who looked cranky and stilted. The quality of craftsmanship might not be high, so it might not be viewed as a lovely work of art. If this were the case, the portrait essentially would be dead, much like its sitter.

Looked at as material culture, however, the portrait can be used as a wonderful interpretive tool to describe a particular woman—the sitter. If she is known, research can reveal details of her life and the portrait can be used as a visual focal point for a great interpretive story. Most directly, the portrait might be the single most vibrant way to introduce a particular woman who lived at a particular moment in time. The portrait invites a guide to give the sitter's name, her background, her interests, and her role within the household, if the setting is a historic house.

If the sitter is not known, the portrait still can be used to inform a discussion about the lives of women generally at a particular period of time. For example, the woman's tightly curled hair might offer a vehicle to discuss personal hygiene and hairstyles at the time when she lived. Her steady, tight-lipped expression could also provide an opportunity to compare the formality of sitting for an oil painting with the informality of a snapshot taken with a camera. When looked at as material culture, the portrait encourages questions of guides and visitors alike.

> ***Historical message:*** *A portrait encourages lots of valuable questions: What did the sitter want people to know about her during her own lifetime? What did the sitter want posterity to know about her? What does the painting tell us about this person,*

and what does it say about women generally at that time? How would her life experience compare with that of women today?

These types of questions are essential in historic site interpretation. They enhance a site's historical message because they use material culture as physical evidence that supports important ideas and themes. Good questions asked of material culture potentially draw connections that engage the visitor. They also have the potential of placing the site within a larger context.

❖ Remember: *A successful interpretive tour compares the past with the present and explains the difference. Material culture offers visual links and clues that facilitate these comparisons.*

How to "Read" an Artifact

Purpose: To give guides practice in how to analyze and interpret the material culture at your site.

Time: Forty-five minutes

Preparation: Review Reading 5.2, *Asking Questions of Material Culture,* assigned in Activity 5.1, step 10.

Assemble materials

Choose five or six pieces of material culture, *in situ,* that illustrate one or more of the site's interpretive themes (be sure to include significant architectural or landscape features, as well as two-dimensional objects, such as maps or manuscripts). Familiarize yourself with each artifact and the "five steps."

Photocopy Worksheet 5.1, *Five Steps to Interpret Material Culture.*

Procedure:

1. Lead a brief discussion about the assigned reading, Reading 5.2, *Asking Questions of Material Culture.* Encourage questions and comments to be sure that everyone understands what material culture is. Once the discussion is completed say that it is time to put the ideas into action, using the material culture at the site.
2. Take the guides to one of the selected objects. Distribute Worksheet 5.1, *Five Steps to Interpret Material Culture,* and review the questions on it:

   What is this object? *(identification)*

   What did it do? How was it used? *(function)*

   Who made it? Who used it? What meaning/importance did the object have for people in the past? *(people)*

   What are the relationships among the object, its function, and the people associated with it? *(ideas)*

   What connections can we make between the story of this historical object and our own lives? *(interpretation)*
3. When finished with the demonstration object, move to another and talk the class through the procedure, again using the worksheet as a guide.
4. By now the group should understand the process. Divide the class into small groups. Assign one of the remaining objects to each group. Give the groups ten minutes to analyze their objects and apply the five-step procedure by completing the worksheet.
5. Reconvene the class. Ask each group to present their object and its analysis to the whole group. Encourage discussion about the presentations to ensure that all five steps have been adequately addressed.

Five Steps to Interpret Material Culture

Step 1: What is this object? *(identification)*

Step 2: What does this object do? How was it used? *(function)*

Step 3: Who made it? Who used it? What meaning/importance did the object have for people in the past? *(people)*

Step 4: What are the relationships among the object, its function, and the people associated with it? *(ideas)*

Step 5: What connections can we make between the story of this historical object and our own lives? *(interpretation)*

Material Culture in a Historic House Setting

Purpose: To give guides practice incorporating historical context into discussion of material culture evidence in a period space or in the landscape. To encourage guides to be selective and discuss only those objects that have rich interpretive possibility.

Time: Sixty minutes

Preparation: Assemble materials

Photocopies, Worksheets 5.1 and 5.2, *Five Steps to Interpret Material Culture* and *Using Material Culture to Build an Interpretive Tour*

❖ *Make clean copies of Worksheet 5.1*

Select five or six objects, each in a different space at the site. Choose objects that illustrate significant themes that the site interprets.

❖ *Choose obvious examples. This will reinforce the fact that guides must be selective about which objects they discuss when they give their own tours.*

Procedure:

1. Divide the class into groups and give them twenty minutes to complete the assignment. Distribute Worksheets 5.1 and 5.2. Assign these three tasks:

   A. *Analyze* the assigned object, then complete Worksheet 5.1.

   B. *Consider* the object within its physical context, then complete Worksheet 5.2, which asks the following questions:

   - What is the relationship of this object to its room or exterior setting?
   - What does the object "say" about that space?
   - How can the object be used to interpret its space and the site to the public?

   C. *Prepare* a short, two- to three-minute interpretation of the space using the object as a key illustration of a significant theme or story. Be sure to link the object with a historic person at the site and include any important contextual information.

   Now, take each group to their particular room or exterior space and identify the object they will examine. Float among the groups as they work and answer questions as needed.

2. Reconvene the class and start a tour of the examined objects and spaces. Move sequentially around the property and have each group make its presentation. (Progress from exterior sites to interior spaces, using a path that mirrors a typical tour route.) After each interpretation, encourage comments and questions. Reinforce how different groups successfully used objects as physical evidence illustrating key themes at the site. *Applaud* interpretive efforts.

Using Material Culture to Build an Interpretive Tour

Using the information compiled in Worksheet 5.1, examine your object in its setting and answer these questions. *Short phrases or a list of key ideas is fine. Use the back if needed.*

1. **What is the relationship of this object to its room or exterior setting?**

2. **How can this object be used to interpret the space it is in?**

3. **What background information (context) do you need to provide so that visitors will understand this interpretation?**

4. **How can this interpretation of this object contribute to the overall interpretation of the site?**

5. **Prepare a two- to three-minute interpretation of this historic space using the object as a key illustration of a significant theme or story. Link the interpretation to at least one historic person important to the site.**

CHAPTER 6

Interpretive Themes and the Thematic Tour

HISTORIC SITE GUIDES ABSORB MANY FACTS, IDEAS, AND SCATTERED pieces of information about architecture, material culture, people, genealogy, the landscape, and historic lifestyles. Guides may learn specifics about how people cooked, handled firearms, dressed, slept, or operated machinery. They also may gain perspective on larger, contextual issues such as gender roles, how the workplace changed over time, or how people have defined home and family. With all this information and all these ideas, guides know so much that they potentially can give many different tours of the site. This can be good. Sites need guides who are flexible and can adapt the tours they give to the needs and interests of their visitors.

Still, all this information can pose a challenge. **Guides cannot tell visitors every fact and idea they have learned.** Simply stated, this will be *too much* for visitors to absorb and remember.

Rather than try to tell visitors *everything*, a historic site should identify the important ideas that make the site special and memorable. By focusing on these significant ideas, or *themes*, sites can offer tours that present a lot of information in a clear, structured, organized way. Tours built on themes, reinforced with vivid, documented stories and striking physical evidence, will help people learn and remember important messages about the site. **Thematic tours** are well-organized and built on solid research. They serve both the site and its visitors because they interpret history in an engaging way that is accessible to a broad public. Starting with the activities in this chapter, guides will learn about the site's interpretive *storyline* and its related *themes, physical evidence (material culture), biographies (the "people" stories),* and *historical context*.

By using these building blocks—*the storyline, themes, physical evidence, biographies,* and *historical context*—guides can give rich, interesting, and memorable *thematic tours* of the site.

GOALS

- Guides will learn and understand that a **storyline** is the narrative "plot" that summarizes the most historically significant information about the site. The storyline has been considered and developed by the professional staff and others to unify the site's interpretive and public programming. It has a beginning, a middle, and an end, just like a short story or movie plot. A storyline lends coherence to the information presented at the historic site and it helps people to remember significant *ideas* rather than lots of disconnected facts.

- Guides will learn and understand that a **theme** is a statement or idea that illustrates and expands an important subplot within the storyline. A theme is the message you want visitors to carry away.

- Guides will learn that **physical evidence, the site's material culture**, both documents and illustrates major themes.

- Guides will learn how to look at the site from the **various perspectives and biographies** of the different people who lived, worked, and visited there over time.

- Guides will learn and understand that **historical context** is the background information that visitors should know in order to understand the site's storyline and themes. Historical context considers the larger picture of how the site fits into events and trends within American economic, political, social, and cultural history.

- Guides will learn that **a strong storyline, themes, physical evidence, biographies, and historical context are the essential building blocks for structuring meaningful tours of historic sites**. Theme-based tours help visitors make sense of and remember what they have seen and heard at a historic site. To give a theme-based tour, guides must gradually internalize the site's storyline. Then they must know where and how this storyline is best illustrated at the site.

- Guides will **understand how a thematic tour outline is created and organized.**

- Using the thematic tour outline, guides will **learn how to develop interpretations for specific spaces** using architecture, landscape features, biographies, and two-dimensional and three-dimensional artifacts as evidence to support the site's interpretive themes.

- Guides will understand that **a tour outline is not a script**. It is a skeleton that a guide fleshes out to create a well-organized tour, tailored to the needs and interests of particular tour groups.

- Guides will learn how to **flesh out the tour outline**, and will experiment with using it to create varied tours suitable for varied audiences. Guides will become skilled in using the thematic tour outline for the site and will **practice** giving thematic tours for one another.

- Finally, guides will know **how *not* to give a tour.**

An *interpretive tour* is

not a rambling description of the passing scenery
not a running monologue of the genealogy of the owners and occupants of the site
not a catalogue of beautiful things and decorative arts jargon
not a series of seemingly random facts
not a recapitulation of everything the guide has learned about the site
not a memorized script

TRAINER PREPARATION

- Before training guides to give interpretive tours, the site should **complete the activities outlined in part 1**. In summary, these activities require the site to:

  Write a storyline. This is the summary "plot" of the interpretive tours that guides will give. A storyline offers a short, but compelling narrative incorporating the themes chosen by the site. This document serves as the foundation for the site's interpretation and programming.

  Identify and articulate three to five themes central to the site and its historical significance. Themes are "big" ideas that support the site's storyline.

  Establish the historical context that offers essential background information visitors must have to understand the site's storyline and themes. To summarize this information, **prepare a time line for the site.**

  Identify physical evidence central to the chosen themes. This requires locating key objects and locations on the site, then linking them with the themes.

  Identify and prepare biographies for key historic figures associated with the site. Also prepare a genealogical chart or other summary that identifies the key figures associated with the site and their relationships with one another.

  Write a three- to five-page summary history of the site, integrating the main themes and the various forms of evidence that illustrate them.

  Create a thematic tour outline for the site.

  Photocopy the site's storyline, themes, summary history, biographies, genealogy chart, time line, and thematic tour outline.

- **Review the concepts** defined in Reading 2.1, *Storylines, Themes, Physical Evidence, Biographies, and Historical Context: Definitions and Examples.*

TRAINING STRATEGY

- **The recommended training activities in this chapter are adapted from those used during the roundtable workshop.** They are designed to introduce the concepts of *storyline, topics, themes, physical evidence, biography* and *historical context* so that guides will be familiar with the terminology and ideas associated with thematic tours. The activities will help guides *own* the building blocks required to create a thematic tour.

The trainer should be careful, however, to avoid having the class rewrite the site's storyline, themes, historical context, and thematic tour outline. Rather, the trainer should encourage the group to embrace the storyline and themes that the site has created and accepted as part of the roundtable workshop activities. **The activities in chapter 6 are designed to accomplish this while teaching guides the strategies and techniques of giving thematic tours.**

- **Lead the class through a series of discussions and activities that will help them design an excellent thematic tour of the site.** Though the staff has prepared a thematic tour outline, encourage class members to think independently as they participate in discussions. The more participatory the activities, the more people will invest in the ideas and strategies essential to a strong thematic tour.
- Encourage the class to think of the tour outline as a skeleton or foundation that they will flesh out in their own way. ***Remember:* Each guide should use the tour outline to build their individual interpretations and tours.** Though every tour should address the major points of the tour outline, encourage the class to develop a personalized approach to the material. This can be accomplished by choosing evidence or adding information that reflects the interests of the guides.

TRAINING ACTIVITIES

ACTIVITY 6.1

Thematic Tours vs. Non-thematic Tours

Purpose: To teach guides the difference between a thematic tour and a non-thematic tour.

Time: Sixty minutes

Preparation: The trainer knows the storyline and themes of the historic site. The trainer has developed a thematic tour of the site and can demonstrate it, or parts of it, to the class.

Procedure:

1. Divide the class into pairs or small groups and request that the groups not consult one another. Ask each group to develop a three-minute presentation of a period space (parlor, bedchamber, kitchen, etc.). Give each group a slip of paper that identifies the particular non-thematic focus their tour should have, for example:

Location	Focus
Parlor	**Decorative arts**: discussing artifacts as works of art
Kitchen	**A process**: giving a step-by-step description of the way food was cooked, or how latches were made, or how pigs were slaughtered
Bed chamber	**Gossip**: offering juicy stories about people connected to the site
House façade	**Astonishing facts**: presenting lots of facts, statistics, and judgments of quality ("this is the best, or the biggest, or the oldest widget in the country")
Dining room	**"Pots and Pans"**: identifying objects, one by one, in the room

   Give the groups about ten minutes to develop their presentations. Have each group assign one member to give the tour.

2. Have each group give their presentation, moving from period space to period space in a logical sequence. After each presentation, ask the whole group to recall what information was presented and, if possible, identify the overall focus of the tour.

3. Return to the same spaces. As the trainer, give a short, thematic presentation of each space. These brief tours should use biographies, artifacts, structures, architectural features, and the landscape to convey a message linked to the storyline and themes adopted by the site. Ideally, the presentations will be lively and engaging, and focus on "people stories."

4. Lead a wrap-up discussion of the various tours. Consider these questions:

   How were the presentations different?

   Which offered the most meaningful interpretation?

   Which kind of presentation does the best job of teaching history?

   Can you distinguish the themes? What are they? How do you know?

   How/why does the thematic tour work?

An Introduction to the Components of a Thematic Tour—Storylines, Themes, Physical Evidence, Biographies, and Historical Context

Purpose: To familiarize guides with the building blocks of the site's new thematic tour.

Time: Thirty minutes

Preparation: Assemble materials
Photocopies, Reading 2.1, *Storylines, Themes, Physical Evidence, Biographies, and Historical Context*

Procedure:

1. Distribute Reading 2.1, *Storylines, Themes, Physical Evidence, Biographies, and Historical Context*. Give the participants time to read it.
2. Open a discussion about the reading. Discuss how each of these components contributes to a strong thematic tour. The goal is to help the class to *learn* and *remember* that:

   A *storyline* is the narrative "plot" that summarizes the most important information about the site.

   A *theme* is a sentence or two that conveys a significant message that you want visitors to learn and remember.

   The *physical evidence* is the site's unique *material culture* that both documents and illustrates the main themes.

   Historic people shaped the site and their *biographies* greatly enrich the stories that can be told. It is important to understand the various perspectives of the different people associated with the site in order to build a well-rounded interpretation.

   Historical context is the background information that visitors will need to know in order to understand the site's storyline and themes. Historical context provides the larger picture of how the site and its story fit into general patterns of American economic, political, social, and cultural history.
3. Ask if anyone has any questions. Close by asking the class to insert the reading into their training notebooks so that it will be available for reference for the remainder of the course.

ACTIVITY 6.3

The Storyline

Purpose: To introduce and discuss the primary story of the historic site.

Time: Fifteen minutes

Preparation: Assemble materials
Photocopies of the *site storyline* developed by the staff

Procedure:

1. Review what a storyline is: specifically, a storyline is similar to the plot synopsis for a movie or short story. It summarizes in narrative form what is important and memorable about the historic site. It underpins and informs all forms of interpretation at the site, including guided tours, publications, exhibitions, special programs and events, and multimedia presentations.
2. Distribute the storyline adopted by the staff after the roundtable workshop. Ask the class to read it. Ask the participants to underline or highlight the most important ideas in the storyline. Then ask them to identify and discuss its narrative thread. Encourage questions and comments. Lead a quick and informal discussion about why the storyline is important and how it can help guides frame their own thematic tours.

ACTIVITY 6.4

Historical Context—Discussion

Purpose: To identify important historical information that visitors will need to know for an interpretive tour of the site to be meaningful.

Time: Thirty minutes

Preparation: Review the site time line and summary history

Procedure:

1. Ask the class to turn to the site time line and summary of the site's history, both of which are in their training notebooks. Give them five to ten minutes to review both, encouraging them to underline or otherwise indicate those ideas or pieces of information they find especially important.

2. Open a discussion. Ask the class to identify facts or ideas that are required "background knowledge" for visitors to understand the specific history of the site. This list should be wide-ranging. For example, some information may be basic:

   at Gettysburg, visitors must know that the Civil War occurred between 1861 and 1865, and that this pivotal battle occurred in July 1863

   Some may be more general:

   during the late nineteenth century many Americans benefited from rapid improvements in plumbing, central heating, and electricity

   Some may be somewhere in between:

   this Southern plantation, like most large Southern plantations, depended on the labor of enslaved African Americans

3. On flip-chart pages, list the facts and ideas mentioned by the class. Keep the conversation flowing by encouraging the class to recall what they learned from lectures and other presentations about site specifics given at the outset of the training course. Encourage a conversation about which pieces of background history now appear to be most important for visitors to know. Ask the class if it has enough information about this background. If they need or want more background, be prepared to suggest additional reading or ask if there is a volunteer who would like to prepare a short report.

❖ *Consider this discussion as a conversation sparked by ideas drawn from reading and learning. Open-ended discussions such as this add variety to the learning process and encourage people to link "big ideas" with specific facts. Such discussions also help people begin to articulate some of the ideas that they will later incorporate in their tours.*

Finding the Site's Topics

Purpose: To identify and prioritize the *topics* associated with the site.

Time: Thirty minutes

Preparation: Assemble materials
Easel, flip chart, and markers

Procedure:

1. Introduce this activity by explaining that the group will discuss important *topics* associated with the site. A topic is a noun or short phrase that is not embellished by a description or additional information. It is a fact from which a theme can be built. (Examples of topics include the *Revolutionary War, Georgian architecture, indoor plumbing,* and *plantations.*)
2. Present several topics developed for the site during the roundtable workshop as examples. Open a discussion, asking people to think of additional topics related to the site. List these on flip-chart pages.
3. Ask the group to look at the flip-chart pages. Have them begin to prioritize the various topics. Which topics seem most important when considering the historical significance of the site? Which may be less important but still have interpretive significance? Which are least important for visitors to know?
4. Encourage continued discussion. Gradually move toward consensus about those topics that are most important for understanding the site. Write the selected topics on a new flip-chart page. Tape these pages to a wall in preparation for Activity 6.6.
5. Conclude with a brief wrap-up discussion to assure that there is consensus among the group about the topics they have chosen.

Identifying the Site's Themes

Purpose: To help participants understand how a theme is constructed. To introduce the site's themes and help participants use the themes to interpret a variety of important topics.

Time: Thirty minutes

Preparation: Assemble materials

Flip-chart pages of site *topics* generated in Activity 6.5, taped to the wall or otherwise visible to the group

Flip chart and markers

Photocopies of the three to five themes for the site developed during the roundtable workshop

Procedure:

1. Remind the group that a theme is a fully developed sentence that conveys an idea. A *theme explains* what is important about the topic and *develops* it into a message that the site wants visitors to hear and remember. Give examples of topics expanded into themes, using either examples developed for your site during the roundtable workshop or the examples below, which are pertinent to the Caleb Crawley House:

   The Revolutionary War marked the end of colonial America's dependence on Mother England and the beginning of national political and economic independence.

   Georgian architecture relied on formal designs based on symmetry, balanced proportion, and elegant decorations that reflected the ideals of the Age of Reason.

   Women's education in the eighteenth century was uneven. Wealthy females learned reading, writing, arithmetic, and occasionally French. Most girls were restricted to learning only rudimentary book skills. All girls learned to sew, cook, and manage households.

   As white American males declared their independence in 1776, large numbers of **enslaved Americans** lacked the freedom to choose their place of residence, vocation, and way of life.

   American individualism is entwined in America's sense of itself. From the earliest days, settlers on the frontier sought opportunities to better their lot in life.

   The birth of American manufacturing in the eighteenth century helped break the country's dependence on imported British goods and led to the full-scale industrial revolution that occurred in the nineteenth century.

   Chinese export porcelain was popular among wealthy Americans during the eighteenth century.

   Ask the participants if they have any initial questions about the difference between a *topic* and a *theme*.

2. Distribute photocopies of the three to five themes identified during the roundtable workshop, refined by the staff, and adopted by the site. Encourage questions and comments.

3. Write each theme on the top of a flip-chart page. Review the list of topics developed in Activity 6.5. Work to link the more significant topics to the themes. As consensus is reached, write the topics under the relevant theme(s) on the flip-chart pages. Discuss how the themes and topics might be used together in an interpretation.

Historical Biographies: Interpreting Multiple Perspectives, Part 1

Purpose: To help guides develop a historically accurate, yet creative approach to the site, presenting it from the various perspectives of people who lived or worked there at a particular moment in time.

Time: About two hours

Preparation: Assemble materials

Photocopies of the short biographies developed for the site and Worksheet 6.1, *Interpreting Multiple Perspectives: People, Places, Objects, and Themes*

Procedure:

1. Distribute the short biographies and Worksheet 6.1, *Interpreting Multiple Perspectives: People, Places, Objects, and Themes,* to each person. Divide the class into groups, assigning a historical character to each group. Allow time for everyone to skim their biographies and the worksheet. Ask if there are any questions.

2. Ask each group to spend a few minutes reviewing the worksheet to identify the space on the historic site where they will work. Tell the groups they will have about twenty minutes in the space to complete the worksheet and develop a short interpretive tour of the space they have selected. Tell them to be prepared to give a tour of this space to the rest of the class, presenting it from the perspective of their particular character.

   ❖ *Allow the class to give the tour in either the first-person voice or the third-person voice. For example:*

   First person: *"Hello, my name is Rachel and I am the cook for the Crawley family. Let me show you around the kitchen as I begin to prepare dinner. . . ."*

   Third person: *"This is the kitchen where Rachel, the cook for the Crawley family, made all the meals. Rachel's first task each morning was to make sure there was a fire in the fireplace. . . ."*

   Agree to meet as a whole group at a specified space on the site to begin the tours.

3. When the groups have completed their worksheet and prepared their tours, meet at the specified space. Have the corresponding group give its tour. Move to the second space for the next tour and continue sequentially around the site until each group has made its presentation. After each tour, ask questions, for example:

   Did the tour successfully communicate the point of view of the historic character about the space?

   Did the tour address what the person did within this space, using physical evidence to support the interpretation?

   Did the tour consider the person's relationships with other historic characters within this space?

   Allow time to consider how other historic characters might have used, or not used, the space. For example, if a group just presented a cook in the kitchen, ask:

   What might the mistress of the house have done in this space?

   Would the cook and the mistress have talked?

   What space within the kitchen might each have occupied?

When interpreting the space associated with the mistress, ask similar questions:

Would the cook have been here?

Would she and the mistress have talked and if so, about what?

The goal is to encourage the class to think about the site from the point of view of particular characters, and then to think about the whole site as a place where many people lived, worked, played, and interacted. Move through each of the prepared interpretations, encouraging comments, questions, and suggestions, and noting that the activity will be developed at the next session. Ask the class to bring their completed worksheets, *Interpreting Multiple Perspectives: People, Places, Objects, and Themes*, to the next training session.

Interpreting Multiple Perspectives: People, Places, Objects, and Themes

Character name:

Who was this person? (List a few facts that reveal something about the person's background, personality, role within the household, work, etc.)

Where on the site would this person have slept?

eaten?

worked?

entertained?

What objects on the site might this person have used? (Name a few. Be specific.)

Where are they? (Cite the spaces.)

Are there spaces or objects that this person would never have used? (Give a few examples.)

What was the relationship of this person to other people who lived on the site or visited it?

Does the story of this character illustrate a theme or themes of the site? If so, which theme(s)?

NOW: take this information and go to the space that *best* illustrates this character. Choose a few objects that support the story of this character. Develop a short interpretation of the character, using the space and chosen objects as an illustration of how this person used this space. If possible, link it with a theme of the site. The goal is to try to think of this space from the point of view of the person who occupied it many years ago, then present that person's perspective to a modern audience. ***For example**, the perspective of a male owner of the house toward the parlor would be quite different from the perspective of the maid who dusted it.*

ACTIVITY 6.8

Interpreting Multiple Perspectives, Part 2

Purpose: To develop the ideas and interpretive strategy introduced in Activity 6.7.

Time: About three hours

Preparation: Class has brought the completed Worksheet 6.1, *Interpreting Multiple Perspectives: People, Places, Objects, and Themes.*

Procedure:

1. Lead a brief discussion about the experiences of Activity 6.7, focusing on how different spaces can be used to tell the story of particular historic characters at the site. Ask if there are any questions based on the activity. Answer and discuss as needed.

2. Ask the groups formed in Activity 6.7 to reconvene. Then ask each group to prepare a half-hour tour of the site, presented from the perspective of the character they have been assigned. They may choose spaces and objects as they desire. Encourage the groups to include at least one space where their character would have spent *less* rather than more time. This will assure a well-rounded consideration of how the person used the site as a whole.

   Tell the class to think hard and try to "see" the site as their character would have seen it.

   Urge them to find strong and interesting ways to present that point of view to the public.

   Stress that the tour must incorporate the site's interpretive themes, utilize the material culture, and be a fully developed presentation with a beginning, a middle, and an end.

3. Tell the groups they have one hour to prepare and practice their tours. Ask everyone to return to the training room in an hour.

4. As the various groups move around the property to prepare their tours, circulate to make sure they stay on task and to answer any questions.

5. When the groups have prepared their tours, have the class reconvene. Then, pair groups and ask that the paired groups give their tours to each other. Encourage them to refrain from comments or questions until both groups have given their full tours. Ask that the groups return to the training room at the conclusion of their tours.

6. Lead a brief discussion about the experiences the class has had. Ask some questions:

   Were there any particularly compelling interpretations, where a space and a person sprang to life?

   What comparisons did the tours generate?

   Were there aspects of this type of interpretation that seemed difficult or awkward?

   Were there devices about this activity that can be applied to more general tours of the site? If so, what?

   Are there particular characters who emerge as unusually compelling "spokespeople" for the overall interpretation of the site?

   How did this activity enrich, or distract from, the kinds of interpretations individual guides are developing for the site?

Using the Evidence to Communicate Themes

Purpose: To provide experience in applying themes, material culture evidence, and "people stories" to the interpretation of specific spaces at the site.

Time: About ninety minutes

Preparation: Assemble materials
- Flip chart, easel, and markers
- Extra copies of the site's storyline and themes
- Photocopies of Worksheet 6.2, *Using Evidence to Interpret Themes*

Procedure:

1. Ask the class to list significant spaces for interpretation at the site, including building exteriors and the landscape. Encourage them to think of *all* the places where they might interpret a piece of the site's story to the public—the entrance, front parlor, stair landing window, the kitchen, a vegetable garden, the barn, a vista from a porch. Record these sites on a flip chart.

2. Divide the class into several groups. Assign each group one of the interpretive spaces identified in step 1. Encourage the class to refer to Reading 2.1, *Storylines, Themes, Physical Evidence, Biographies, and Historical Context,* in their training notebooks and to the site time line.

   ❖ *If there is not a group for every interpretive space identified by the class, assign those spaces that have the richest interpretive potential. Make sure that sections of the landscape are included.*

3. Distribute Worksheet 6.2, *Using Evidence to Interpret Themes.* Ask everyone to review it to see if they have any questions. Send the groups to their individual spaces, telling them they will have forty-five minutes to complete the worksheet. Ask the groups to reconvene in the training room after they have completed their task. Circulate among the various groups as they work, to assure that they understand their assignment and to answer any questions. Help them keep track of time, giving them a reminder when their forty-five minutes are about to expire.

4. When the groups return to the training room with their completed worksheets, ask if there are any questions about the activity.

5. Ask one person from each group to read or present their interpretation. Be sure to say that this is not the time to evaluate the interpretation. The goal is to see how the site's physical evidence and historical biographies are used by the groups to communicate the themes.

6. After each group has presented their interpretation, open a discussion about how physical evidence and historical biographies work together to support and enhance the communication of the storyline and themes.

WORKSHEET 6.2

Using Evidence to Interpret Themes

Name of space:

Key theme(s) of the site illustrated in this space:

Physical evidence (one to three examples) that illustrates this theme:
Note: *This can include architectural or landscape features in addition to artifacts*

How can this physical evidence be used to interpret one or more people associated with the site? (Make a few notes or an outline for reference.)

NOW THINK: Are there other objects or characters that are so interesting in this space that they require some attention, even if they do not connect with the identified theme? If so, have you chosen the *best* theme, *best* objects, and *best* character to talk about in this space? Is it worth reconsidering your choice of themes and evidence? Is it possible to talk about this other object or character in ways that are interesting but do not undercut the most important information or message identified for the space?

NOW: Pull it together to create a summary statement. Taking the historic space, the two to three objects, and the historical character you have chosen, develop a short, interpretive paragraph that uses them as evidence illustrating a key theme of the site. Think of this statement as a short story with a beginning, a middle, and an end. Think of the objects as "evidence" and the historical character as the "star" that together reinforce and enhance the story's meaning. (Use the back of the worksheet for notes, if needed.)

NOW: Develop an interpretive tour of this space. Using the theme(s), physical evidence, historical character, and ideas on this worksheet, develop a short interpretive tour of this space. Practice it several times, giving different people turns. Refine it and be ready to give it to other members of the class.

Practice, Practice, Practice

Purpose: To provide the class with the opportunity to learn, then practice the new thematic tour outline so that they become comfortable with it.

Time: Three to four hours, depending on the length of the tour and size of the class

Preparation: Assemble materials

Photocopies of the *thematic tour outline* developed by the staff in part 1

Procedure:

1. Distribute the *thematic tour outline* developed by the staff. Give everyone a few minutes to review it.
2. Open a discussion about the outline. The class should see that the key spaces they have been interpreting comprise important sections of the overall outline. What the full outline includes are lots of the missing links:

   a place for an *introduction* and general directions

   transition spaces

   secondary spaces with less central interpretive messages but still part of the general movement through the site

   a place to conclude the tour

   Ask the group to spend a few moments to imagine this tour—its sequence, its messages, its overall flow. Ask for comments or ideas, but stress that this is the outline that will underpin most thematic tours of the site.
3. Tell the class it's time to test their skills and build their thematic tours. Divide the guides into pairs. Give the pairs a few minutes to meet and review the outline to assure that there are no substantial questions or problems.
4. Once everyone is comfortable with the thematic tour outline, ask each pair to work together to develop a tour using it. Give them a few minutes in the meeting room to take notes, if needed, but encourage them to get out onto the site as soon as they are ready. Ask the guides to take turns giving a tour to their partners using the new tour outline. Encourage them to think of this as valuable practice time and the opportunity to flesh out their tour in a personal way. Tell them it's all right to make mistakes and reassure them that though at first they may feel awkward giving a tour to a peer, this is a great way to get support and positive feedback. Provide these guidelines:

   One partner should complete the entire tour before the second person begins.

   The listener's role is to be attentive and offer constructive, supportive comments to the person doing the tour.

   The listener may also serve as a sounding board for any questions or concerns the guide has about her own tour (content) and delivery (personal style).

   ***Remember**: teams work as partners, helping and supporting each other.*

   ❖ *There are two ways that this activity can be organized to assure that each interpreting team has space:*

   Option 1: If possible, do this activity when the site is closed to the public to maximize the space where the guides may work. If the class is small, stagger the starts so that everyone begins at space 1. If the class is large, start each pair at a different spot on the site. Ask each pair to begin *(welcome and introduction)* and end *(closing comments)* their tours at the same spot, making a circular route.

❖ *If the groups must be staggered they necessarily will follow a different route from the one prescribed in the tour outline. Help them by writing out the new route for them. Encourage them to be flexible because situations like this often arise if large groups visit the site.*

Option 2: If it is not possible to do this activity when the site is closed, or if the site is too small to accommodate many groups, ask the guide pairs to do the activity on their own within a specified time (perhaps a week). With this option, have people log in when they are doing their tours and ask them to take notes about any problem or suggested changes they have for a future discussion.

5. Reconvene the guides after they have given their practice tours. Ask how the tours went and discuss their reactions. Ask for any suggestions about the tour outline that might improve it or make it more effective. Ask what worked and what was less successful. Encourage them to share tips with one another. Take notes and discuss any suggested revisions with the site staff.
6. Provide opportunities for guides to practice and polish their tours. Encourage guides to practice until they feel comfortable giving tours based on their tour outline.

CHAPTER 7

Communication: *Audience and Presentation Techniques*

A GREAT THEMATIC TOUR OUTLINE IS ONLY HALF THE CHALLENGE of giving visitors an excellent interpretation of a site. The other half, just as important, is the *guide's personal communication style*. The very best tour outline will fail if it is not well presented. Good guides must be adaptable, confident, pleasant, and capable of reading the needs of their audience. They must know how to use their voices and even their bodies in ways that further and do not distract from the presentation. In short, learning to be a good guide—like learning to be a good public speaker or storyteller—requires an understanding of the elements of effective communication, the skill to respond to the needs of audiences, and the means to identify and improve upon individual communication weaknesses.

When we humans communicate, we send both verbal and nonverbal information to listeners. In order to communicate successfully, we must be able to dissect our own performances, to see how we use verbal and nonverbal cues to convey messages. By analyzing our own presentations, and looking at them as visitors might, we can identify what works, recognize and change what needs improving, and cultivate an effective personal style.

Another important part of the communication equation is the listener. Good communicators are adept at "reading" their audiences, gauging their needs, and responding to their interests quickly. Effective guides are flexible and know how to adjust their tour to make it more compelling for their listeners. Interpretation is strongest when a guide's communication style and presentation technique connect in effective ways with the audience. Simply stated, ***good communication skills*** **plus** ***good history*** **equals a** ***good guided tour.***

The variety of activities in this chapter are designed to help each guide develop an effective personal communication style. The activities will encourage each person to

Understand the *components of communication*
Make a frank *assessment of their individual strengths and weaknesses*
Develop the *skills* required to understand the needs of diverse audiences
Introduce *techniques* that can help with both verbal and nonverbal communication

These activities, however, must be viewed as only a beginning. Effective presentation of any sort requires practice and lots of it. Encourage guides to practice on their own, alone, and with their peers and friends. The more comfortable guides are with their presentation style, as well as with the tour outline and route, the greater the likelihood that they will give great tours.

GOALS

- Guides will consider the presentation and impact of the tour from the audience perspective.
- Guides will understand that people learn in different ways.
- Guides will identify their own communication strengths and weaknesses.
- Guides will practice listening and observation skills.
- Guides will understand the process of communication and be able to analyze their role in that process.
- Guides will identify strategies for working with different kinds of audiences and different kinds of people in a tour group.
- Guides will practice elements of communication, including the effective use of voice and gesture.

TRAINER PREPARATION

- Identify the audiences who come to your historic site. Most sites enjoy visitation from a broad, general public: people of different ages, sexes, races, and special needs. Often tours have a mix of people, but special tours are just as common: a class of seventh graders, an Elderhostel group, a group with physical or mental challenges. If the site has conducted visitor surveys that analyze attendance, share the results. Lacking formal surveys, review sign-in books and talk with experienced guides and the site educator to develop a general profile of who comes to the site. *Help* guides be ready for *all* the people they will see.

- Review the suggested activities and choose those that fit your site's needs. The activities are divided into two general categories—*audience strategies* (7.1–7.7) and *techniques* (7.8–7.9).

- Identify and schedule lecturers on specialized topics that fit your site's needs and the interests of your class. Examples include how to work with the physically or mentally challenged, strategies appropriate for young children, and learning-style theory as applied to historic sites and museums.

TRAINING STRATEGY

- The activities will help guides step into the shoes of different kinds of visitors and experience the tour from their perspectives.

- Discussions will help guides develop strategies to work with different kinds of audiences with various special needs.

- Emphasize that **excellent communication is essential to every type of presentation**. A tour, no matter how strong the content or organization, is successful only if it is communicated in an effective way.

- **Good communication skills can be taught,** but like acting or a musical performance, they require practice to improve. Good communication skills can be practiced every day, not just with the prescribed activities in this chapter.

- Good communication skills increase the likelihood of a positive response from an audience. In turn, when an audience responds well it usually shows and this makes the performer feel great. **Good communication skills make giving tours more fun** as well as more interesting for visitors.

Field Assignment—Taking a Tour

Purpose: To sensitize guides to the needs of their visitors by having them become the audience.

Time: *This activity has three parts*: the *assignment* (which should be piggy-backed onto the immediately preceding training session), the *tour*, and the *follow-up discussion*. The assignment should take about ten minutes to explain, the tour length will be variable, and the discussion should take about thirty minutes.

Preparation: At the conclusion of one of the previous training sessions, briefly present the *assignment* (below) and schedule a follow-up *discussion*. Allow enough time (at least several weeks) for guides to take their tours of another site. Photocopy Worksheet 7.1, *Taking a Tour from the Audience Perspective*, for distribution at the assignment meeting.

Assemble materials

Flip chart, easel, and markers

Assignment

1. Ask the trainees to take a *guided tour* of another historic site of their choice in your area. Give them several weeks to do this and encourage them to partner with another trainee to encourage discussion about their shared experience. Encourage the class to visit a variety of places, as this will lend a broader perspective to the subsequent discussion. Set a date for a one-hour meeting to discuss observations made during these tours.

2. Direct the class to take their tours as if they were casual, "off the street" visitors. Stress that the purpose of the field study is to focus on the visitor's perspective, not to sit in judgment on the guide. If there is no guide and the tour experience is intended to be self-guided, encourage the interpreters to consider how the site conveys its messages and whether these devices are effective. Suggest that at some point during their visit they try imagining that they are a child, or an elderly person, or one who has difficulty hearing, seeing, or walking.

3. Distribute Worksheet 7.1, *Taking a Tour from the Audience Perspective*, to focus observations. Tell the class they should fill it out *after* the tour; it should not be visible during the tour. The comments on this worksheet will help shape the follow-up discussion.

4. People should identify sites and tour times on their own. Be available for questions or recommendations about good places to visit.

Discussion

1. Have each guide team identify the site they visited and give a *brief* description of their experience. Then, have them address the particulars on the worksheet with the overall goal of identifying common problems (what didn't work) and common strengths (what did) on the various tours.

2. Encourage a discussion of *useful* techniques or strategies that can be applied at your own site. Expect comments such as:

   There was a crying child on my tour and the guide was terrific in the way she handled it. She. . . .

   Our guide had the greatest way of starting the tour. She said. . . .

   There was an older person on our tour who had trouble hearing, so our guide. . . .

   Our tour group included a family with kids who ranged from a fidgety five-year old to a bored thirteen year old. Our guide did a great job including them in the tour because she. . . .

   Note the responses on a flip-chart page.

3. Ask what didn't work on tours. Expect such answers as:

    The guide only spoke to one person who was especially receptive. The rest of us eventually felt left out. . . .

    The guide kept jingling change in his pocket and it drove me crazy.

    The guide used big words that little kids didn't understand.

    The guide just pointed at the furniture and told us what it was.

   Note the responses on a flip-chart page.

4. Now ask the class to look at the list of "problems" and urge them to suggest solutions or alternatives that would have improved the situation. Note these responses on a flip-chart page.

5. Ask the class to look at all the information culled from their tour observations. Lead a short discussion to help the group begin to make some generalizations about their tour experiences that can be developed into a handy tip sheet for easy reference. Ask for a volunteer to draw up the tip sheet and then distribute it at the next training session.

   ❖ *Remember, while the negative is always fun (this list will be long), your real goal is to establish those specific steps a guide must take to assure that visitors have a positive experience at your site.*

Taking a Tour from the Audience Perspective

Use the following questions to focus your observations and think about the visitor experience on the tour you take. Jot down your notes *after* the tour, then compare with your partner.

Who was in your group or visiting the site at the same time as you? How many people were there? Ages? Any observable special needs?

How did the guide size up the people in the group? (Did she ask where they were from, inquire about their interests, accommodate particular needs?)

Were you encouraged to ask questions, share ideas?

What was the balance between the guide talking and the visitors participating or looking on their own?

Did you get the right amount of information—too much, too little?

What accommodation would someone with special needs require for the tour to be enjoyable and rewarding? (Special needs can range from being an energetic nine-year old to being physically or mentally challenged.)

Did the guide employ useful techniques to make her tour more successful? Describe.

How did the guide end the tour? Was it effective?

What was the most memorable story you heard or experience you had at the site? What made it memorable?

Based on your experience, would you recommend the site to other visitors? Why or why not?

ACTIVITY 7.2

A Communication Model

Purpose: To establish an intellectual framework for understanding the complexity of the communication process. How does it work? How can it fail? How can we avoid a breakdown in communication?

Time: Thirty minutes

Preparation: Assemble materials
Flip chart, easel, and markers
Photocopies, Reading 7.1, *Good Communication Skills:* Tips for Guides

Procedure:

1. Draw the following communication model on the flip chart

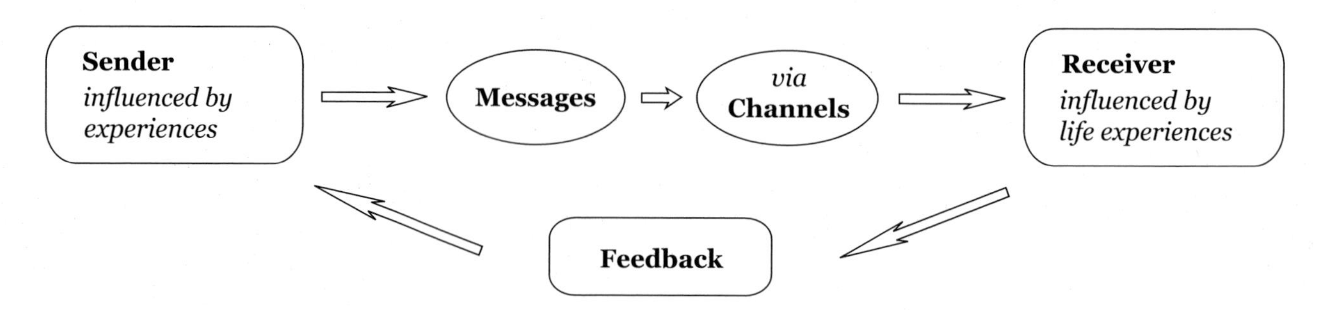

2. Explain that this diagram summarizes how communication occurs.
   - **Communication is a process in which a person, group, or organization creates a *message* and *sends* it through a *channel* to a *receiver*,** who could also be a person, group, or organization. Both the sender and receiver are affected by life experiences, which can include personality traits, training, knowledge, feelings, health, and even their reactions to one another. Usually a sender creates multiple messages and sends them through several channels. The receiver decodes the messages based on his/her life experiences and sends feedback.
   - In a tour, **the *sender* is the guide. The *message* is the tour content**—which includes information about the site and its organization. The ***channels* include the guide's words, nonverbal communication (gestures, labels), and the physical evidence** of the site. **The *receiver* is the visitor.**
3. Discuss some possible causes for breakdowns in communication between the sender and the receiver. List these on a flip chart. Examples include,

   ***Sender*:** the guide is ill or unhappy, biased, cranky, pressed for time, or lacks knowledge

   ***Message*:** it may not be age-appropriate, or the content may be poorly organized

   ***Channels*:** the tour may be too long or boring, the group too large, or the space may be noisy

   ***Receiver*:** the visitor may already have had a long day, have tired feet, have impatient children, or be there under duress
4. On the flip chart, write *"sender," "message," "channels,"* and *"receiver,"* leaving ample space for writing under each. Then ask,

   How can a sender avoid breakdowns in communication when difficult situations arise?

Note responses on a flip chart. Then ask,

How can we be sure our messages don't break down in their communication?

Note responses on a flip chart. Then ask,

What can we do to make sure our channels work for us, and not against us, and if they are against us, what steps can we take to turn the situation around?

Note responses on a flip chart. Then ask,

How can we be attentive to the needs of the receiver to assure the best possible experience for him or her?

Note the responses on a flip chart.

5. Lead a brief wrap up discussion allowing people to share more ideas or comments. Distribute Reading 7.1, *Good Communication Skills:* Tips for Guides. Encourage the class to review it and refer to it as they develop their tours.

❖ *This activity adapts a training strategy developed by Margaret Piatt.*

Good Communication Skills: Tips for Guides

A solid, well-organized tour outline is only half of the challenge of providing a positive experience for visitors. The best tour outline, if poorly presented, can fail if it is not presented well. Strong content must be matched with a strong presentation. Keep these communication skills in mind when working with the public:

1. **Speak slowly and clearly**. Use vocal and facial expressions to enliven the presentation.
2. **Avoid jargon and slang.** Avoid annoying but often unconscious habits such as jingling coins in a pocket or clicking a pen.
3. **Maintain good eye contact** with all members of your group, from the oldest to the youngest.
4. **Encourage questions**, but don't pressure people to respond, as they may feel like they are being tested.
5. **Be receptive to people's interests** as indicated by questions or information provided prior to the tour. Tailor tour content to reflect these interests.
6. **If someone asks a question that you can't answer**, say you will find a curator or other expert on the site to help obtain more information. Follow through on this at the end of the tour.
7. **If someone touches an object**, walks where they should not, or otherwise breaks site protocol, address the problem politely yet firmly. It often helps to say, *"we work hard to preserve our site and ask that nobody, including staff, touch our objects."*
8. **If there is an emergency**, stay calm and follow site protocol. If the guide is calm, visitors will be more likely to stay calm as well.
9. **Be sensitive to any special needs in your audience**, whether hearing or vision difficulties, the different attention spans of children and adults, or physical challenges.
10. **If a visitor becomes unruly** or disruptive, be polite but firm in requesting that they respect the needs of the other visitors and the site.
11. ***Remember,* you are the warm, engaging person who makes personal contact with visitors**. Visitors tend to remember their guide as much as the specifics about the site. Be a great ambassador and you will create a positive and memorable tour experience for visitors!

Adapting the Message to the Audience

Purpose: To help guides identify the characteristics of various visitor groups and practice adapting the site message to suit visitors' needs.

Time: Forty-five minutes

Preparation: Assemble materials
- Paper and pen for each group
- A completed photocopy of Worksheet 6.2, *Using Evidence to Interpret Themes,* for a specific room in the house

Prepare slips of paper, each naming a different type of visitor group (for example, a couple, fifth-grade students, several family groups with mixed ages, senior citizens). There should be one slip of paper for each group.

Procedure:

1. In the classroom, divide the guides into groups of three or four. Give each group the completed photocopy of Worksheet 6.2, *Using Evidence to Interpret Themes,* some paper, and a pen. Give each group a slip of paper with the name of their "visitor" on it. Ask each group to identify typical characteristics for their visitor. These should be informational, not judgmental. Have someone note these characteristics on a piece of paper.
2. Still in the classroom, ask the groups to create a hypothetical, five-minute tour of the assigned space that is appropriate for their assigned visitor. (Use Worksheet 6.2 as a reference.) Ask each group to focus on communication techniques rather than the specifics of information. These should consider gesture, facial expression, and good use of voice. Have them practice to be ready to demonstrate it to the rest of the class.
3. Reconvene the class and ask each group to identify their visitor group, then demonstrate their interpretation. Ask them how they made decisions about what to say and how to say it. Encourage general conversation about strategies that work well with particular kinds of audiences. Some strategies to consider include:

   Asking questions of the visitors*: What strikes you about this space? Have you ever wondered how people kept their food chilled two hundred years ago?*

   Comparing and contrasting objects and ideas of the past with those of the present. *This is effective with most groups, as it links the past with the immediate experiences of the visitor. It can be especially effective with students, who are by nature more interested in the present day than the distant past.*

   Role playing*: acting out a particular story in a first-person voice, whether the voice of a servant, the owner of the house, or a child.*

   Using gesture or voice to help people understand*, especially if they have vision or hearing impairments.*

   Employing hands-on activities to reinforce messages*. These usually require reproduction props, but can be a wonderful way to engage people of all ages and interests.*

4. Identify strategies that may not work as well with particular groups, giving reasons and examples, if possible. Examples include:

   Asking adult groups lots of questions*. Many adults are uncomfortable if they feel they are being put "on the spot." A few questions can be effective, but know when to stop. Be especially cautious asking lots of questions of senior groups. Hearing difficulties can make this approach difficult and uncomfortable for the visitor.*

Role playing *can be effective with children and mixed groups that instinctively know that children require a bit of entertainment with their education. Role playing may be far less successful with a senior group or group of adults who prefer a more straightforward presentation.*

Comparing the present and the past in nonparallel ways*. If the historic site was the home of a rich person, it is important to keep this economic distinction in mind. When pointing out a carriage, for example, do not say, this is the way people traveled a long time ago. Most people in fact did not. It would be more accurate to say, this is how rich people traveled a long time ago. Most of us would have walked or had a wagon. Owning this carriage would be like owning a limousine or other luxury car today.*

Lecture-style tour*. This may work well with groups who have highly specialized interests, such as decorative arts or a particular period of history. Generally, however, it is less successful with all other kinds of groups.*

5. Encourage the group to brainstorm about effective strategies to work with a relatively common tour situation: a mixed group that includes children and older adults with special needs. The goal is to encourage the guides to develop a flexible approach that will potentially let them employ several different styles within a single tour. If the class is interested, consider doing a role play where a guide can practice making strong eye contact with elderly people who may be hard of hearing, then quickly turning to a child, making eye contact at his level, and pointing out an object that will have particular appeal (a toy, a funny picture, a hands-on opportunity). If the brainstorming proves useful, summarize the ideas on a flip chart and ask a volunteer to develop a guide's tip sheet that can be distributed at the next training session.

Working with People of Different Ages—Children, Adolescents, and Adults

Purpose: To help guides recognize that people of different ages learn differently and relate to the environment around them in different ways. To encourage them to "read" their audience just as they have learned to read material culture.

Time: Sixty minutes

Preparation: Assemble materials
Photocopies, Reading 7.2, *The Five Stages of Human Learning:* Tips for Guides.

Procedure:

1. Distribute copies of Reading 7.2, *The Five Stages of Human Learning:* Tips for Guides. Give the class a few minutes to read it. Ask if there are any questions or brief observations about the material.
2. Ask the group to begin to focus on learning-style characteristics that they have noticed about particular age groups: children, adolescents, adults, and senior adults. Record this information on a flip chart.
3. Divide the guides into small groups and assign them a particular age audience: children, adolescents, adults, senior adults. Encourage them to think about the different learning styles and methods of presentation that might work with each of these age groups.
4. Have each group spend ten to fifteen minutes identifying a fuller list of characteristics for their assigned audience. Then, based on these characteristics, ask each group to brainstorm and develop a list of "tour tips" for forming successful interpretation strategies for this audience.
5. Send each group, with their interpretive strategies in hand, to a different space at the site (parlor, bed chamber, outside the front door, etc.). Give them fifteen to twenty minutes to develop a short but effective interpretation of this space for their assigned audience. (This will require both mastery of the site's story line and themes, and conscious choices about presentation techniques and interpretation strategies.) Encourage each group to brainstorm, develop a general approach for their audience, and then develop a sample tour, which they should practice, both as interpreters and as the audience.
6. Ask each group to present their "age appropriate" interpretation to the rest of the class. (Ask the rest of the class to imagine they are the age group being addressed.) After each tour, informally discuss what worked, what didn't, and what improvements might be made to present the site better to given audiences.
7. Conclude the session with a general conversation about specific techniques that work for particular audiences and how certain of these strategies can be applied to general tours of the site. Again, it may be useful to list ideas on a flip chart that can then be summarized in a guide's tip sheet.

The Five Stages of Human Learning: Tips for Guides

In their book, *The Good Guide,* Alison Grinder and Sue McCoy summarize the five major stages of human learning. Understanding this developmental sequence greatly aids the content and presentation style that can be most effective for different age groups. The phases and their characteristics are:

1. **Age three to six: egocentric perspective**

   Children's perceptions revolve solely around their own ideas and perspectives. They do not understand that other people will have different points of view.

   Tour style: an emphasis on simple identification of objects with their names.

2. **Age five to nine: subjective perspective**

   Children begin to recognize that others have different perspectives, usually based on observation of behavior, but generally they are unable to understand or anticipate what these different perspectives might be.

   Tour style: a storytelling approach of a dramatic event. Questions that reinforce important information and describe the actions different people took in different situations.

3. **Age seven to twelve: self-reflective thinking perspective**

   Children understand that other people have different perspectives, feelings, thoughts, and values. They begin to think subjectively about their own behavior.

   Tour style: a storytelling approach with added questions that encourage children to think about what they would have done in particular situations.

4. **Age ten to fifteen (early adolescence): mutual perspective**

   Adolescents understand their own perspective, that of another person, and that of an abstract "third person," which allows them to make generalizations about larger groups of people.

   Tour style: a thematic tour that presents important ideas about the site and adds questions about *why* these ideas are important.

5. **Age sixteen to adulthood: in-depth and societal perspective taking**

   Adult thinking coordinates multiple perspectives to create a larger social view. This includes an understanding that people analyze their own experiences based on their own perspectives.

   Tour style: a thematic tour that incorporates historical context, the multiple perspectives of various historic characters, and linkage with contemporary life.

❖ *This reading is based on Alison Grinder and E. Sue McCoy, The Good Guide: A Sourcebook for Interpreters, Docents and Tour Guides (Scottsdale, Ariz.: Ironwood, 1985), 32–35. Their summary is based on the findings of Swiss psychologist Jean Piaget and subsequent work by Robert Selman, who categorized how children perceive and interact with the world around them.*

Special Needs Audiences

Purpose: To familiarize guides with a variety of special visitor needs so that they can give confident, gracious, and informative tours.

Time: Variable, but the typical session is about one hour

Preparation: Identify, make available, and assign pertinent readings from the bibliography.

Schedule special speaker(s) as desired.

Assemble materials as needed for particular activities:
Flip chart, markers, wheelchair, petroleum jelly, cotton balls

---

Procedure: There are a variety of ways to introduce guides to the needs of special audiences. Choose one or more of these options as time and interest permit.

Some Options

1. Hold a general discussion about the many different special needs audiences who might visit your site. Discuss particular strategies, note them on a flip chart, and then develop the material into a guide's tip sheet.

2. Schedule a lecture by a teacher, person with special needs, or social worker affiliated with a school or other institution that serves a special needs audience (for example, a school for the blind or for children who have cerebral palsy, or a social welfare agency serving local residents with physical or mental challenges). Ask the presenter to leave ample opportunity for questions. The chief goal is to give your guides as much information as possible so they can handle any situation that arises with both knowledge and grace.

3. Divide the class into teams of several people each. Have one person in each group assume the role of a special needs visitor. Props that can help simulate relatively common special needs include a wheelchair, balls of cotton inserted into ears, a blindfold, or petroleum jelly smeared onto eyeglasses. Assign roles to each person in the group: a guide, a special needs visitor, and general visitors. Ask people to think about a tour from the perspective of their assigned role. Then, as a group, discuss ways to give a successful tour that answers these needs. Reconvene the groups and lead a break-out discussion where each group shares the ideas, strategies, and tips the exercise prompted.

4. If your site does not already have a policy on visitors' or other site emergencies—sudden illness, accident, screaming child, fire—develop one. Present and discuss your emergency policy with the guides so that they are familiar with the procedures and options available to them. Hold a brainstorming session about strategies for specific situations. Make a guide's tip sheet and distribute it.

Interpreting Sensitive Topics to the Public, Part 1

Purpose: To help both *new* and *experienced* guides feel comfortable with topics or issues that are often sensitive for modern audiences (e.g., slavery, the Holocaust, mental illness, child labor). To encourage discussion about how to handle difficult situations that may arise.

Time: Forty-five minutes

Preparation: Assemble materials

Background reading material on appropriate historical context

Photocopies, Reading 7.3, *Interpreting Slavery at Historic Sites:* Tips for Guides, or a similar tip sheet developed by the site that addresses an important but potentially sensitive topic

Carefully review the suggested *trainer preparation* prior to scheduling this class. Additional research and preparation may be required, depending on the materials about the topic that are currently available at the site.

Trainer Preparation:

1. Become familiar with the historical context related to the site. Review pertinent material about topics that are important to the site's history and interpretation but can be difficult for the guide or the audience. Consider how these aspects of the site's history contribute to a fuller and more balanced understanding of the site, its region, and the nation.

2. Assemble all the site-specific research that is available about the topic(s). If necessary, expand this resource with additional research. For example, if addressing slavery, examine site documents to see if there are references to slaves in general or to specific individuals. Check courthouse records for census or probate information. Try to identify the name(s) of people so that the discussion can focus on the experience of a real person.

3. Prepare a packet of readings for guides that includes both contextual information and some primary sources. Develop a tip sheet for guides that presents information about the sensitive topic and offers ideas about effective ways to present the topic to the public. See Reading 7.3, *Interpreting Slavery at Historic Sites:* Tips for Guides, as a model.

4. Examine the site's material culture and identify spaces and collections that can be used to discuss the topic(s) and the people connected with it. This sometimes requires looking at objects or spaces from multiple perspectives and asking questions. Who prepared food and how did they do it? Who cleaned, emptied chamber pots, tended children, and plowed fields? What did this work involve? Consider arranging furnishings in a room to invite discussion about the labor required to maintain a household. For example, show a dining table in the process of being set for a large dinner. A reproduction straw pallet in a bedroom could help spur discussion of the slave who tended children twenty-four hours a day.

5. Consider creating interpretive devices to show what can no longer be seen on the site: photographs of factories and living conditions in the city from which the grand estate was a retreat; reproductions of servants' or slave clothing that can be compared with that of the house owners; photocopied documents (letters, records from an account book, lists of slaves) that can be shown to visitors. Choose images, objects, or documents that amplify the site's thematic messages.

Discussion:

1. Open a discussion with both experienced and new guides. Emphasize that the site's responsibility is to educate as well as entertain. State that the institution is committed to interpreting its themes, which include this sensitive topic, and that it expects guides to incorporate what may be

new material. A good way to introduce this is by saying, "As a result of new research, we will be revamping the tour."

2. Emphasize that knowledge is the guide's best offense and defense. Guides do not need to be experts, but they should know how to get more information if visitors ask questions they can't answer. They should feel comfortable saying, "I don't know, but I'll ask the curator at the end of the tour," or, "We don't know the answer to that question, but we are working on it." However, if a guide is asked *how* she knows how many slaves were on the plantation, it is important that she can state the source for her information (a document, archaeology, new research, etc.).

3. Encourage guides to share their concerns and discomfort. Then encourage guides to devise strategies for addressing problems that might arise.

4. Distribute the tip sheet(s) developed about this topic or topics. Open a discussion about the issues raised in it.

5. Adapt activities from chapter 5, Material Culture: *The Physical Evidence*, and chapter 6, *Interpretive Themes and the Thematic Tour*, to help guides to include and be comfortable with discussing slavery, child labor, war, etc.

6. Involve guides in the development and training of the new interpretation. Guides involved with the planning can help anticipate potential problems, and because they are fully invested in the process, they can play a significant role in leading discussions and training activities for other guides.

Interpreting Slavery at Historic Sites: Tips for Guides

Adapted from materials developed by Beth Taylor, director of interpretation, Montpelier, a historic site of the National Trust for Historic Preservation

1. **Integrate history**
   Slavery and race are central to an understanding of American history. Get away from the "add-on" approach. Develop a holistic tour, integrating the subject of slave life into the mainstream interpretation of the site.

2. **Interpret with direction**
   Time is precious, so set interpretive objectives. Presentations should be designed to support particular themes or messages you want visitors to carry away with them.

3. **Provide context**
   Give visitors the historical background they need to appreciate the site's interpretation. Keep learning yourself. Know your sources and share them with visitors.

4. **Present a balanced view**
   Slavery is a story of horror but also a story of human strength and survival on the part of the African Americans who experienced it and who maintained their humanity despite the inhumane system.

5. **Emphasize the individual**
   Seek opportunities to convert "slavery" into the story of the men and women who endured it. Slaves were individuals with individual responses to the system. Help visitors appreciate their multiple perspectives.

6. **Face race**
   A full and honest treatment of slavery eventually requires taking on the complex topics of race and racism. Increase your comfort level with discussing these complex issues a little at a time.

7. **Embrace complexity**
   Avoid pat answers. Increase your tolerance for complexity and help your visitors do the same. The search for historical "truth" is a tentative, ongoing exploration shaped by the historical circumstances of the present.

8. **Enliven your presentations**
   Don't lecture at people. Use artifacts, features, and spaces actively and creatively, as springboards to ideas. Enliven presentations through theater or archaeology. Try using the inquiry method, drawing visitors out with questioning techniques. "How do you think slaves coped?" or "How might slaves have resisted?"

9. **Promote diversity in the staff and in the site's audience**
   Seek out multiple points of view. A diversity of participants generates stimulating, thought-provoking ideas.

10. **Seek out mentors and models**
    Pair with experienced interpreters of the African American experience. Invite speakers to the site. Visit other sites where slavery is interpreted.

Interpreting Sensitive Topics to the Public, Part 2

Purpose: To build greater comfort and confidence in guides

Time: Forty-five minutes

Preparation: Assemble materials
3 × 5 cards

Procedure:

1. Introduce the activity by saying that it is natural for guides to feel uncomfortable about how to present new and potentially sensitive material to the public. Say, too, that it can be challenging to respond properly to certain situations or questions.

2. Give each guide a 3 × 5 card and ask that they complete the following statement: "I would be more comfortable talking about (topic) if. . . ." Tell people to be honest! Make sure they know this is a safe place to talk about complicated issues and what could well be conflicting personal thoughts about the topic. Say that the comments will be kept anonymous and the cards will be thrown out after the training session. Give everyone a few minutes to write their answers.

3. Collect the cards to preserve anonymity. Ask someone to read them aloud. Note the key phrases on a flip chart. If there are repeats, indicate with a star or check.

4. Open the floor for discussion. Ask people to elaborate on the concerns raised by the class as a whole. Allow plenty of time to acknowledge the validity of people's comments. Expect answers such as these, genuine responses given at sites addressing the question of slavery:

   I knew that the research and sources I was referring to were current.

   I wasn't afraid to say something insensitive.

   I was sure I had the support of my supervisor.

   There were no African Americans in my tour group.

   I knew what to do about negative visitor reactions.

   I knew stories of specific people at my site and how they related to the history of the area.

   In some cases the comments will identify additional research that should be conducted to support the guide giving the tour. In other cases, the comments will point up personal discomforts associated with presenting sensitive topics. In these cases, allow guides to brainstorm solutions about how to overcome anxieties. If the group as a whole seems unusually anxious, consider having pairs of guides role play good ways to address particular situations such as:

   discussing slavery with a mixed group of people who include two African Americans

   answering a belligerent question about "winning the west" and the slaughter of Native Americans

   explaining controversies revolving around the display of Native ceremonial objects

   responding to other controversies explored by exhibits at historic sites or museums

5. Ask everyone to review Reading 7.3, *Interpreting Slavery at Historic Sites:* Tips for Guides, or its equivalent developed by the site. Open a discussion and ask if there are additional suggestions that should be added to the tip sheet to make it more helpful. Take note of these and at a later date distribute a revised tip sheet.

Voice

Purpose: To help guides improve the ways they use their voices

Time: About forty-five minutes

Preparation: Assemble materials
Flip chart, markers

Choose and photocopy short sections from famous speeches (from history or literature). You will need a different speech for each guide

Practice the exercises in this activity and be prepared to lead the class through them. Alternatively, find a voice or drama coach to lead these exercises.

❖ *Remember that many people feel self-conscious doing this type of activity. It will help the class feel more self-confident and relaxed if you are self-confident and relaxed yourself. Stress that these exercises do help with voice projection, enunciation, and overall vocal clarity, which helps ensure effective communication.*

Procedure:

Explain that this class will focus on five exercises that teach elements of good vocal technique: relaxation, proper breathing, resonance, phonation, articulation, and expression. Explain that it is possible to train voices to assure good communication. Understanding and using good vocal technique helps guides speak effectively and safely, enabling them to maintain vocal health despite hours of relatively heavy use. The voice and diction exercises that follow should be practiced at home until proper breathing and phonation are second nature. (Many of the exercises will be familiar to those who have sung, done extensive public speaking, or acted.)

Exercise 1: Relaxation

Good vocal technique begins with learning how to relax muscles in the face, tongue, jaw, chin, throat, and neck. Unnecessary tension in these muscles may interfere with good speech.

1. Sit in a comfortable and relaxed position in a chair that supports your back.
2. Gently stretch your neck muscles. Use your hands to gently massage the muscles on either side of your neck, from ear to shoulder.
3. Gently massage the muscles of the face and throat, starting at the hairline. As you stroke, allow the facial muscles to go limp.
4. When you get to your chin, pause, and hold it between your thumb and forefinger. Move your jaw gently up and down—slowly at first, and then rapidly. DO NOT use your jaw muscles to move your jaw; let your hand do all the work.
5. Pay attention to how these muscles feel when they are fully relaxed. Although you will use many of these muscles for articulation, it is important to know what the relaxed state feels like so that you can avoid tensing muscles unnecessarily.

Exercise 2: Breathing

Breath carries tone, so good vocal health and effortless speaking depend on proper breathing. Though breathing is an involuntary action, the techniques of proper breathing for speech are not all involuntary or second nature. Good breathing can be learned.

1. Start with good posture. Stand with your feet apart to hip width, knees slightly bent, and spine aligned. Your neck should be relaxed, head erect, chest slightly raised, and pelvis "tucked."
2. The goal is to use your diaphragm, and not just the upper chest, while breathing. The diaphragm is a muscle that separates the chest cavity from the abdomen. It is shaped like an inverted bowl. When the lungs fill, the diaphragm flattens. When this happens, the abdomen moves outward. We can see and feel this happen, which helps us monitor breathing technique.
3. To practice diaphragmatic/abdominal breathing, first establish good posture, with a slightly raised chest.
4. Place one hand on your chest and the other on your midriff. Exhale, maintaining your posture and chest position.
5. Inhale slowly through your mouth, keeping your chest and shoulders still. Think about sending air toward your abdomen. The hand on your midriff will be pushed outward by the air, but the hand on your chest will not move.
6. Exhale, but do not allow your chest to collapse.
7. Continue breathing slowly in this way, making sure to keep your chest and shoulders still, for ten full inhale/exhale cycles. Then relax. Repeat.

❖ *If you have trouble getting the hang of diaphragmatic/abdominal breathing, try this. Lay down somewhere and relax as though you are about to go to sleep. As you relax, your body will use diaphragmatic breathing automatically. See what this feels like; it will help you when you practice.*

Exercise 3: Resonance and Phonation

A resonant voice is full and rich, and projects easily and comfortably. *Resonance* is a product of *phonation*: the sounds our voices produce (phonation) that are amplified in the bones and cavities of our heads (resonance). By learning good use of our resonators, we can maximize our natural capacity for resonance and produce the most sound with the least vocal strain. We can also manipulate our resonators to change the color and impact of the sounds we produce. Like an actor who can produce many different "voices," we can learn ways to produce sound to increase emphasis, enhance storytelling, and add emotional effect.

1. Stand with proper posture (see exercise 2, step 2). Relax the muscles of your face and neck. Inhale and exhale several times, using diaphragmatic breathing.
2. Take a deep breath and let out about half of it. Interrupt the exhale with a light, singing sound on "hah." Begin in the upper middle of your voice range and allow the pitch to slide downward. Keep your throat relaxed and chest slightly elevated while doing this.
3. Repeat the exercise, but this time allow your lips to close and open lightly several times. The result will be a pitched "m" sound, much like a hum, in between the "ah" sounds. Keep the throat and neck relaxed and the air moving, even when your lips are closed.
4. Now use the same downward inflection punctuated by "m," but change the vowel sounds. Start with "hah," then move to "meh," "mi," "moh," and "moo." Keep the breath moving, chest raised, and throat relaxed.

5. Now switch to the phrase "how are you," still using sliding downward pitches. Do it in a "sing song" fashion, with the vowels elongated—like the vowels in the previous exercises. (Do not speak the words in a normal fashion.) Try this starting high, low, and in the middle of your range, but always be sure your voice is relaxed and that you are breathing properly.
6. Divide guides into pairs and ask them to do the "how are you" exercise for each other. The listeners should check for proper posture, good breathing, and relaxation in the neck and face. Then, standing five to six feet away from the speaker, they should listen to the sounds produced in the different parts of the speaker's range. Finally, they should listen for the sounds produced while the speaker says the different words. In what range does the voice sound clearest? Loudest? Most relaxed? The guides should give constructive feedback to one another and try again, aiming for a full, relaxed, resonant sound.

Exercise 4: Articulation

Although most pitch and tone are carried on vowel sounds, we must use consonants to create articulate speech. Good articulation, sometimes called "enunciation," requires the *proper* use of consonants. Without good articulation, speech can be garbled and difficult to understand. This is extremely frustrating for listeners. In contrast, well-articulated speech is easy to follow. The following two exercises combine the skills learned above and add practice in articulating consonants clearly.

1. Start with good posture and a relaxed face and neck, and establish solid diaphragmatic breathing.
2. Take a deep breath, and while exhaling say:

   Mama's a mean mama, papa's a poor papa, baby's a bad baby

   These silly phrases are very useful in learning good articulation. Listen for the clarity of the words, but don't allow the muscles of the mouth, jaw, or tongue to get tight. Keep your voice relaxed.
3. Establish good posture, relaxation, and breathing as described above.
4. Use a sentence or two from a famous speech as an articulation exercise. Say the sentence and experiment with different pitch levels to find where it sounds and feels best. Play with this a bit until you find just the right place in your voice to speak the sentence. Then, exaggerate the articulation. While doing this, concentrate on enunciating so that every word can be understood separately. Do not slur or be sloppy with the consonants.
5. Divide the guides into pairs. Ask the partners to practice their sentences with each other, aiming and listening for the fullest, most relaxed and clearly articulated speech.

Exercise 5: Expression

Speech without expression is flat and boring. The inflection and emotional intensity we add to our phonation and articulation helps keep listeners engaged. We use expression all the time in our everyday speech. Think how many meanings the simple question "what?" can have, depending on its inflection. It can convey a range of emotions: confusion, annoyance, or pleasure. Like actors and storytellers, all public speakers can benefit from planning effective expression. In the best of circumstances, expressive speech can be riveting. Try this series of exercises to learn how to use expression in effective ways.

1. Distribute the speech excerpts. Ask the guides to use a pencil to underline those words they want to emphasize to best convey the essence of the excerpt.
2. Have the guides find a place in the room where they can practice their excerpts aloud. Remind them to start with good posture, a relaxed face and neck, and good breathing, and to use resonant, articulate speech.

3. When the guides are ready, split them into pairs. Have them read (or recite) the excerpts to one another, listening for expressiveness. Encourage constructive comments and feedback.
4. Ask the guides to choose an emotion and read the excerpt (or a portion of it) to their partner, trying to convey that emotion. Be sure that the guides DO NOT tell their partners what emotion they are trying to convey. Have the partners try to guess the emotion, then talk about what was most effective in communicating it.
5. Reconvene the group and discuss the various effective ways that emotion was communicated.
6. Conclude the vocal exercises by encouraging the guides to develop their own voice warm-up routines, in which they run through several different exercises prior to giving tours.

Gesture

Purpose: To help guides understand how they use gestures and facial expressions. They should learn how to use these effectively to enhance communication. They also should begin to identify those gestures that may be distracting and should be avoided.

Time: Thirty minutes

Preparation: Assemble materials
Flip chart, easel, markers

Procedure:

1. Organize the guides into pairs. Ask them to take turns telling their partner a simple story, either one they know well or something they make up. The listener should listen to the story, but at the same time she should carefully watch to see how the storyteller uses gesture and facial expression while speaking.

2. Reconvene the group. Ask each person to report one *effective* gesture or facial expression used by her partner. Make sure this information is very specific.

3. Describe the four main types of gestures.

   Illustrative: These are gestures that mimic or illustrate points. They offer an excellent way to illustrate a process. Examples of **illustrative** gestures are:

   Pretending to strike a hammer when describing a carpenter's work

   Moving a hand as if sewing when describing how girls learned to stitch samplers

   Describing the weight of an iron cooking pot by going through the motion of lifting something extremely heavy

   Indicative: These gestures show direction. They are useful in helping visitors understand where to go on a tour. They also help people to get oriented, both on the site and in relation to the site's geographical location. Examples of **indicative** gestures are:

   Pointing in the direction where visitors should walk

   Pointing where a significant landmark on the site is, whether the visitor center, the parking lot, or the river used by the historic residents to travel to the nearest town

   Pointing where, in general terms, the nearest town or city is

   Emphatic: These gestures communicate emotion. They punctuate specific feelings that enliven verbal communication. Examples of **emphatic** gestures are:

   Pounding your fist into your open hand to emphasize an important point

   Raising your arm and using fingers, one-two-three, to reinforce the three main points you want a visitor to remember

   Opening your eyes wide at a dramatic moment in a story

   Autistic: These are gestures we use to give messages to ourselves. They are expressions of how we are feeling. Sometimes we are not aware of these gestures because they are nervous habits. Sometimes they are relatively unnoticed by others. Sometimes they are distracting to others. For this reason, people who do public speaking must work hard to identify and modify any potentially distracting autistic gestures. Examples of **autistic** gestures are:

   Clenching a fist when you are tense or frustrated

   Jingling keys or coins in a pocket while speaking

Fiddling with a button, a purse, a clipboard; clicking a pen

Excessive twitching of the eyes, jerking of the head, awkward movements of the mouth, or repeated clearings of the throat

❖ *Facial gestures can be unconscious and difficult to control. Encourage guides to be as self-aware about this as possible, knowing that sometimes this is difficult.*

4. Point out that illustrative, indicative, and emphatic gestures can be very useful tools that enhance communication. Autistic gestures, on the other hand, often convey negative messages to the public. Recognition of these gestures, however, can help the speaker to identify their feelings, which can aid in easing tension. For example, if a guide realizes she has just clenched her fist, she can pause, take stock, recognize she probably is a little tense, then unclench the fist. Often, by simply recognizing then reversing the autistic gesture, a person can relieve tension. Better to take the moment to recognize the autistic gesture for what it is—a sign of nervousness—than to ignore it. Left unchecked, the tension revealed by an autistic gesture can increase and interfere with effective communication.

5. Discuss appropriate uses for each type of gesture. Discuss examples identified at the beginning of this activity (steps 1 and 2). Seek other examples that arise in tours. Record these ideas on the flip chart. Tell the class that listeners usually mimic a speaker. If a crowd is passive, the speaker can employ more gestures to help enliven the presentation and the crowd. If a crowd appears distracted or nervous, or is noisy, it may be that the speaker is using too many gestures, or using them in a nervous, autistic way that distracts from the messages. If this is the case, the guide may wish to try a calmer, more relaxed presentation style.

   ❖ *This activity adapts a training strategy developed by Margaret Piatt.*

PART THREE

MANAGING GUIDES EFFECTIVELY

CHAPTER 8

Managing Guides Effectively

THE PEOPLE WHO WORK WITH THE PUBLIC ARE AMONG A SITE'S most important resources. Depending on the guide's presentation, visitors can have a lackluster visit or a terrific experience that stimulates good memories, postvisit conversations, and best of all, a desire to learn more. A site must take care of this valuable resource—its guides—just as it cares for its architecture, landscape, and collections. Guides need good training that emphasizes the interpretive goals of the site. They also need good management, supervision, and support to encourage and maintain high-quality presentations and strong morale.

Managing staff can be one of the most challenging aspects of any job. Moreover, managing guides may be only one aspect of a site professional's work. Museum staff, who frequently juggle a multitude of varied responsibilities, can find it difficult to carve out adequate time for staff management. Still, working effectively with guides is essential. These are the people on the front lines. For visitors on a tour, the guide represents the site, what it stands for, and what it has to offer.

In addition to the normal challenges of managing employees, there often are some complicating factors when working with guides. For example, many sites have large numbers of part-time guides who may work two days a week, or two days a month. These part-time schedules can make it difficult to pull people together for training and other purposes. Also, guides can be at different levels of experience, ranging from the recent hire who soaks up every bit of information and is excited about new developments in the site's interpretation, to the guide who has been at the site for years, is an institution herself, and openly resists any changes. (Remember Mrs. Dodge, our guide at the Crawley House?)

Many people who give tours are probably not full-time, paid staff with salary and benefits. They are volunteers or, in the case of guides paid on an hourly basis, nearly volunteer. They work at the site because they find it enjoyable and worthwhile. As a result, they can (and often will) leave if the experience fails to be pleasant and fulfilling. A good management structure provides the framework for an environment in which guides are supported and encouraged to be the best they can be. Good management demonstrates to guides that they are respected members of the museum organization, and sends the message that what they do is important. In this way, guides are far more likely to be successful and happy.

This section of the book presents an approach to guide management that directly involves both guides and site staff in developing policies and procedures. It also relies on using experienced guides as mentors for trainees and new guides. The focus is on developing the specific policies, procedures, and instruments that support the guide's chief task, providing engaging and informative tours. In this context, the most important elements relate to the expectations set out for guides, strategies for ongoing supervision and support, and a strategy for evaluation. Issues related to housekeeping, security, opening and closing, emergency procedures, and other areas of historic house management are not addressed.

Managing guides effectively takes time, energy, and skill, but investing in the effort up front can actually save time in the end.

ADVISORY COMMITTEE ON GUIDE POLICIES AND PROCEDURES

It is useful to assemble an advisory committee composed of guides and staff members who can review the process by which guides are recruited, hired, given ongoing support, and evaluated. In addition to the guide trainer/supervisor, this group might include the site director, curator, educator, director of public relations, and at least two experienced guides. This group may be formed just for this purpose; ideally, it is a standing committee that meets periodically to review progress and discuss issues as they arise.

The advisory committee is important for two reasons. First, when establishing procedures and policies, it is helpful to have the input of people who come at the issues from different perspectives. The result will be stronger than a document created by one person. The "buy in" value is equally important. Participation by guide representatives will strengthen credibility for all guides. The involvement of other staff whose jobs relate to interpretation will contribute to a sense of teamwork across specific job responsibilities. Staff members who are not usually responsible for the guides also will assume more ownership of the program if they are involved in its development.

At some sites, there is a gap between the full-time staff and the often part-time guides. Though thankfully rare, this situation can create tension. This can affect guide staff morale, the presentation of a tour, and ultimately the experience visitors have and remember. At strong institutions, *all* staff members see excellent public service as the site's ultimate goal. This credo makes any barrier between the content specialists and the interpreters more permeable, and assures a textured, well-organized tour grounded in strong scholarship.

HIRING GUIDES

Effective management of guides begins long before a single guide is hired. Careful planning for hiring—including drafting a job description, a list of duties, and a description of qualifications—enables staff and members of the advisory committee to come to a consensus about the different kinds of people who would make good guides. Once these planning tools are in place, effective advertising and recruitment will help the site find candidates. The interview process must also be carefully planned, so that the museum and the candidates have an adequate chance to see if the fit is right. Though good recruits make the best guides, it may not be easy to find the best people. Attracting them requires forethought and effort.

Guide Position Description and Duties

It is essential that the site have a carefully developed and current one-paragraph description of the guide's job. This should be used in advertisements to recruit new guides and referred to when interviewing candidates. The job description provides a framework for the guide's scope of work and a standard against which the guide's performance can be measured.

A good job description lays out the parameters of the guide's responsibilities in a way that reflects the goals of the site. It is direct without being too detailed. For example:

> The guide conducts tours of the *Caleb Crawley House* for the visiting public, interpreting the site's buildings, landscape, and collections in an informative and engaging manner to help the visitor gain an understanding of the site's history and significance. This is a part-time, hourly wage position, limited to an average of twenty hours per week.

To accompany the job description, make a one-page list of specific duties and tasks to be performed by the guide. An example follows.

Duties of the Guiding Staff at the Caleb Crawley House

SAMPLE

1. Guides welcome the public, collect tickets, and direct visitors to facilities, exhibits, and interesting aspects of the site.
2. Guides conduct tours through the house/grounds for visitors of all ages in a personable and knowledgeable manner and provide accurate information relevant to the major themes in the site's history.
3. Guides represent the *Caleb Crawley House* to visitors. They inform them of the site's goals and programs, the need for financial support, and the advantages of becoming a member.
4. Guides assist in providing security for the site, buildings, and collections. They help ensure the safety of the visiting public and respond calmly and professionally to emergencies. They follow institutional procedures.
5. Guides participate actively in training programs and other opportunities in order to expand knowledge of the site and strengthen interpretive skills. Guides are required to update or modify their tours as new or relevant information becomes available.
6. Guides assist with special programs, including but not limited to rentals and special events, often held on evenings and weekends.
7. Guides assist in the office as needed when not giving tours, for example by answering the telephone or doing clerical work.
8. Guides open and close the house, if trained and required to do so.

❖ *If all guides are required to lead programs for school groups, include this in the list of duties.*

Qualifications

Once the advisory committee approves the job description and list of duties for guides, establish the qualifications for the position, including both experience and availability requirements. Emphasize those qualities that are most important for the site, yet be realistic in terms of your community and its resources. For example:

> The guide must have excellent oral communication skills and demonstrated experience working with people. The guide must be articulate, reliable, and have a neat appearance. The guide must be able to assimilate information and impart it in a factual, coherent, and engaging manner, and must demonstrate initiative, leadership qualities, and flexibility. College graduate with teaching experience and interest in history ideal. Guides must be available as scheduled, including some weekends, evenings, and holidays.

Advertising and Recruitment

A good way to recruit guide candidates is to advertise in local newspapers. A short ad for a paid position might state:

> The *Caleb Crawley House* is looking for guides to give tours of the site for the general public. Excellent communication skills and enthusiasm required; an interest in history a plus. A part-time, hourly-wage position, limited to an average of 20 hours per week. Call # ________, ext. ____, for an application.

Ads can be used for volunteer positions, but this expectation must be clearly stated. Newspapers also often will publish press releases or write short stories about the site and its need for volunteers. Other avenues include postings in the site's newsletter and on its Web site, hanging flyers in community facilities such as libraries and senior centers, sending information to area volunteer job banks, and the old-fashioned, but highly effective method of word of mouth.

When a candidate calls, do a brief phone interview. If the person is interested, send an application form, job description and list of duties, and a site brochure. Although resumes can be very useful, requiring one may put off candidates who have strong people skills but little formal background. For example, a good guide might not have a history degree but she may be a highly motivated mother, eager to reenter the workforce after raising small children. Another strong candidate may be a retired salesman who enjoys learning new things and being with people. Form 8.2 provides a sample application.

Paying Guides and Trainees

Paid guides or volunteer? There is no right answer that works for every site; each site has to work within its own resources.

Volunteers have long been the backbone of many historic sites. They work hard, care passionately, and as guides, enjoy sharing their enthusiasm with the public. Typically, however, coordinating many *volunteer guides* requires a proportionate increase in supervision to assure that the site runs smoothly and all positions are adequately staffed. To maintain an excellent volunteer corps a site *must* invest time in professional support and resources such as training materials and programs, guide newsletters, and frequent opportunities for guide recognition.

Many sites are moving toward or already are *paying guides* an hourly wage. This shift reflects the fact that the pool of volunteers is shrinking. A museum or site trying to attract prospective guides may be competing against a variety of community and leisure time activities. At the same time, as sites reach out to broader audiences, they must diversify the staff who greet visitors. Offering a wage may help the site augment the traditional volunteer guide profile of the older white female. The pool of candidates is larger and it is easier to attract a mix of people. For many, the extra income guiding can provide may be very important.

Financial compensation carries a psychological component as well. People *like* to be recognized and compensated for the work they do, and being paid is evidence of being valued. From the site's point of view, an important benefit of a paid guiding staff is the additional commitment people will make. Typically, a person hired as a part-time guide will want to work two, three, or even four days a week, while a volunteer may be available only once every week or two. A group of fewer guides who work more days increases the guides' opportunities to hone skills and bond with each other and the site. There is more contact with the professional staff and better connection with ongoing programs. Paying guides also makes them more accountable. Volunteers serve at their own discretion, and are often more likely to change their availability or resign than people who are paid for their work.

Some sites address the shrinking volunteer pool and a desire to bring in some younger guides by having a mix of paid and unpaid guides. This can work if carefully structured. For example, a site with all volunteers may choose to hire several paid guides to work on weekends, when many of the site's veteran volunteers would prefer to be with their families or traveling.

Should guides be paid for training? Again, circumstances differ widely. Some sites only pay guides when they conduct tours. At these sites, new hires must complete the training process and be deemed ready to give a tour before they are paid. This arrangement presumes that some candidates will drop out before training is completed and the site would therefore lose money. This may be counterproductive. Guide training, like any job training, will be most productive with appropriate compensation for the time involved.

Clearly, a site's financial resources will influence decisions about whether to use paid or volunteer guides. Even if a site has traditionally used a volunteer guiding staff, and that is all the budget will permit for now, it may be useful to lay the groundwork to make the transition to a paid staff. It is important that the site's administration and board know the many ingredients needed to present excellent programs to the public. The quality of the guided tour is as important for the visitor as the condition of the buildings and collections (sometimes more so); creating a budget that establishes what is required to recruit, train, pay, and keep good guides is an important first step.

❖ *Remember: much of the site's success, both educational and financial, rests with the quality of its public programs. Think ahead, plan ways to improve programs and the bottom line, and include in these plans a strategy and budget for training and managing guides.*

Caleb Crawley House Interpretive Guide Application

SAMPLE

Please return to:
 Caleb Crawley House
 Address
 Phone/e-mail

Please type or print legibly

Name: ______________________________

Address: ______________________________

Home Phone: ______________

Work Phone: ______________

Emergency contact: ______________________

Relationship: ______________________

Phone: ______________________

How did you find out about guiding at the Caleb Crawley House?

____

Education

 High School: ______________________

 College: ______________________

 Additional: ______________________

Special skills you bring to the job:

Languages you speak other than English, including American Sign:

Favorite interests, hobbies, activities:

How did you find out about guiding at the Caleb Crawley House?

WORK AND VOLUNTEER EXPERIENCE:

Position	Organization	Dates	Paid/Vol.

The Interview

Once a candidate completes and returns an application form, schedule an interview that includes a tour of the site. Think ahead about the important questions and issues that must be covered, but remember that a good interview is a dialogue. A true "give and take" helps the candidate and the site to learn about one another, clarify expectations, and judge compatibility, interest, and commitment.

Allot thirty to forty-five minutes for the interview itself, allowing ample time for the candidate to ask and respond to questions. Use the interview to welcome the applicant to the site and briefly review the job description and duties. Listen and observe to learn about the applicant's skills, experience, and interests. Make sure that more than one person meets each candidate to provide multiple perspectives. One way to achieve this is to have a guide who serves on the advisory committee give the candidate a brief tour of the site. As part of the tour, ask the guide to discuss what it is like to work at the site and encourage questions and reactions from the candidate. Once the candidate has left, ask the guide for feedback to add to the assessment of the applicant.

ORIENTING GUIDES

Guide Agreement

Many sites require that their guides review and sign a contract or agreement. This signed agreement ensures that the guide understands and agrees to the basic obligations associated with the job, and it puts the guide-site relationship on a businesslike level. This is a brief document. It should not read as a litany of rules.

If a site adopts this policy, *all* guides should sign the agreement—veterans as well as new hires. Asking veteran guides who have worked for years without any formal written document to sign the agreement can be tricky, and some may resist. The request should be presented in the spirit of recognizing the skills and commitment that go into being a guide and placing the relationship on a more professional footing.

Caleb Crawley House Guide Agreement

SAMPLE

Name ____

As a guide at the *Caleb Crawley House*, I understand that I represent the site to the public. I am responsible for:

Guiding visitors through the site, in a personable and knowledgeable manner and interpreting the site and its history to the public.

Following the site's policies and procedures with regard to safeguarding the collections, ensuring that visitors have a safe and enjoyable experience.

Volunteering/working up to _____ hours per month.

Being prompt and reliable in reporting for scheduled work.

Notifying the tour coordinator if I am unable to meet a commitment to the site, and finding a substitute.

Attending required guide meetings and participating in ongoing training activities.

Participating in an annual performance evaluation process.

____ ____________

Guide (signature) Date

____ ____________

Site representative (signature) Date

ESTABLISHING A GUIDE MENTORING PROGRAM

In addition to the advisory committee, a site will benefit by establishing a mentoring program that pairs experienced guides with new guides during the training period. The mentoring arrangement affords new staff frequent one-on-one support from someone who has been through the process of learning the site and the job of guiding. It is often easier to ask questions of a peer rather than a supervisor. Pairing experienced guides with trainees helps the trainees assimilate into the staff and strengthens the sense of connection and communication among *all* guides, no matter what their years of service. The new guide gets high-quality support with less direct involvement on the part of the supervisor, who then has more time to focus on training, supervision, and program-related activities. New guides have a great deal of information to assimilate, often in a short period of time. Mentors provide the guidance, reminders, suggestions, and essential moral support that help new guides to learn their jobs.

Guidelines for the Mentor Program

Identify potential mentors. The best mentors will be guides who are skilled interpreters and would enjoy working with trainees. If the guide corps is uniformly strong, explain the role of the mentor at a regular guide meeting and ask for volunteers. If the skills of the group are uneven, approach the best guides and ask them to consider serving as mentors for new guides. Match mentors with new hires, working to create a good fit in terms of personality and perhaps common interests.

Once selected, meet with the mentors to discuss their responsibilities and the time involved. The most intensive period likely will be the first three or four weeks of training, as new guides become oriented and do their first practice tours. Beyond this, the mentor should expect to work with the new guide periodically for as much as a year. Over time, the relationship between the mentor and new guide will become well established and evolve into a more informal, but still valuable, connection. If guides are paid, mentors should be compensated for this time. If guides are not paid, find ways to offer special recognition, whether by holding a party, giving an award, or writing an article for the site's newsletter.

Mentors should attend the first orientation session for the new guiding class. There they will meet their trainee and the rest of the class, and become familiar with the plans and schedule for the training course. During this orientation, explain how the mentor-trainee arrangement enhances the training process, and review the *Guide Training Checklist, Mentor/Trainee Agreement,* and *Mentor Checklist.*

Guide Training Checklist

It is useful to give new recruits a *Guide Training Checklist,* which enables everyone to keep track of their progress through the training process. After signing the *Guide Agreement,* give trainees the checklist and training schedule. Assign a mentor to the trainee and schedule a time when the two can meet to discuss any questions about the training course or overall requirements to become a fully accredited guide at the site.

Guide Training Checklist

SAMPLE

Name ______________________________ Date ______________

ACTIVITY	DATE
1. Complete employment forms and turn in to the office	______
2. Complete Guide Training Program	______
3. Observe special focus programs	
School Program	______
Family Program	______
Grounds tour	______
4. Instruction in security and maintenance procedures	______
5. Museum Shop Orientation	______
6. Practice Tours	
Practice Tour #1	______
Practice Tour #2	______
Practice Tour #3	______

(Mentor observes first two practice tours, supervisor the last.)

Once this checklist is completed, the guide will be put on the regular schedule.

Mentor/Trainee Agreement

SAMPLE

The Mentor will assist the Trainee by:

- Providing introductions to staff and volunteers
- Reviewing daily operating procedures and policies
- Reviewing resources available for training
- Providing and discussing tour information
- Demonstrating and discussing techniques for handling difficult situations
- Providing information regarding special events, training opportunities, and site issues
- Observing several tours during the first month and periodically as necessary thereafter.

The Trainee will:

- Share progress and concerns with the mentor
- Stay current with site activities through communications with mentor and other staff
- Participate in required training activities
- Evaluate progress by asking mentor to observe tour periodically

❖ *If the trainee and the mentor have a conflict, they will discuss and resolve the issue with the guide supervisor.*

We have read the above conditions and agree to work together from ________________________

to ________________________

____ ____________________

Trainee (signature) Date

____ ____________________

Mentor (signature) Date

FORM 8.6

Mentor Checklist

SAMPLE

Trainee: ________________________________

During the Training Period

_______ Provide employment forms

_______ Review *Guide Training Checklist*

_______ Read, discuss, and sign *Mentor/Trainee Agreement*

_______ Discuss sign-in, lunch, schedule changes, and pay procedures

_______ Introduce trainee to all staff and volunteers

_______ Review ground rules for kitchen use

_______ Tour staff areas, including library (review checkout procedures)

_______ Review Guide Manual, flagging important memos/pages (e.g., security, housekeeping)

_______ Review basic tour techniques

_______ Review what to do during "down time" (e.g., helping education department, answering phones).

After trainee has gone on several tours and attended several training sessions

_______ With trainee, look through supplemental materials (diaries, old photographs, etc.) or explore on-site library to build familiarity with available research resources.

_______ Tour the landscape, pointing out and explaining features and what they suggest about the lives of the occupants. Link this information with the site's themes.

_______ Review information on handicapped accessibility
Make sure trainee knows what can and cannot be done to accommodate handicapped visitors, including what is touchable for blind and sight-impaired visitors.

_______ Talk about duties at special events—when giving stationed interpretation, helping with food service, etc.

On practice tours

_______ Take detailed notes on all aspects of the tour, including factual errors, use of themes, problems with presentation, nervous habits, and handling of visitors. Positively reinforce the good points. Discuss, as needed, areas that can be improved or strengthened.

_______ Explain all notes carefully. Give copies to trainee and to supervisor.

PERFORMANCE STANDARDS AND ASSESSMENT

Conducting a well-thought-out and constructive performance assessment is a critical part of implementing a strong guided tour program. Guides need feedback on a regular basis in order to stay fresh and continue improving their skills. Their job is challenging and quite complex. At the same time, giving a number of tours each week means a lot of repetition, and it is easy to fall into the trap of relying on the same material for every tour. Annual performance assessment helps the guide stay "at the top of her form."

Guide assessment yields several benefits. It establishes a consistent method for monitoring the quality of the guided tour. It can reveal guide achievement, which sites then can recognize in appropriate ways. It can help identify areas in which guides need additional support and training. But, ultimately it is the public that benefits from the guide training program and assessment.

If a site has not previously evaluated guides on an annual basis, or if the process is due for a major overhaul, long-time guides may be resistant and nervous. In some cases, the policy of an annual performance evaluation may even cause someone to drop out of the guide pool. This outcome may be painful for both sides. Sometimes, though, it can provide a graceful exit for a guide who recognizes that she is no longer able to fulfill guiding responsibilities in an effective way. If instituting annual reviews causes extreme reactions among guides, it may be expedient to focus on establishing the standards and assessment process for new guides, and to build in annual evaluation more slowly.

Whatever the timetable, it is important to remember that guides enjoy their involvement with the site most when they are supported in what they do and treated as professionals. Performance evaluation is an important tool that fosters a professional environment.

Guides serving on the advisory committee can play a critical role in developing and reviewing the assessment process. They can be essential allies when presenting the process to the rest of the guide group.

Working with Guides Who Resist Change

Most sites have guides with varying years of experience who have gone through different training programs. Ideally, sites should set aside time for concentrated training and review for *all* guides. Even then, individuals often work at different levels of skill and knowledge. Ongoing training that includes both eager new hires and veteran guides can present challenges that require creative problem-solving. This will be particularly true for those sites that develop and implement new thematic tours that require new training for long-time guides.

Many guides, if treated with respect and kept abreast of new research and ideas about the site's themes, will respond positively to new thematic tours and their required training. For others, this may be more difficult. For example, will Mrs. Dodge adjust to giving the new thematic tour of the Crawley House? Can a plantation site help a guide to stop saying "servant" rather than "slave," or speaking nostalgically about the elegant lifestyle of the plantation owner's family, without reference to the labor upon which that lifestyle was built? Are there ways to encourage a guide to refrain from concluding her tour with the comment about the last owner, "Unfortunately, she never married"? Or can sites steer guides away from a description-based tour and move them toward a thematic tour?

The annual review process outlined in this chapter provides a structure for identifying and discussing issues of performance or attitude with each guide. In addition, sites can develop strategies that will facilitate analysis and reflection about specific problems. *For example:*

- **Change the physical route of the tour.** This helps guides see the site with fresh eyes and is especially helpful when training older guides to give the new thematic tour. A changed tour route also may help a guide to think about specific places on the site from the different perspectives of the various historical people associated with it. Try starting a tour in the landscape and introduce the field hands who tended the crops that supported the lifestyle at the house. Or, start in the kitchen and talk about daily life two hundred years ago. Consider adding a "new" space to the tour by having guides direct a visitor's attention to the stable yard, as seen from a bedroom window, and then develop a short interpretive message that is linked to the site's themes.
- **Create opportunities for guides to work together in small groups** to refine and practice the new thematic tour. This allows them to get to know one another and feel safe about giving each other feedback. If the challenge is to get a guide to drop the old "spiel" and adopt the new themes, use a training session to ask guides to identify the old stories that now must be eliminated.
- Use a few minutes during a training session to **open a discussion about the connotations of words or topics that may be sensitive**. Examples include slavery, servitude, various illnesses, divorce, sexuality, family difficulties, and criminal acts. Use the session to build a collaborative strategy about the right words and right ways to address these sensitive issues. This approach can be more effective than an edict delivered by a site director.
- **Emphasize the importance of representing an institution**. All staff must refrain from offering personal opinions to the public.
- **Offer ways for a person to remain involved with the site, other than guiding, if that has become difficult.** Find ways to make this person feel welcome in a new capacity and present their new job as a new opportunity and not a demotion.

Sites may face dilemmas that require patience. There may be a long-time guide who talks only about the site's objects. This guide may be wonderful with certain special interest groups and can be used accordingly. There are times, however, when a site must bite the bullet. If every effort has failed to encourage a guide to adopt the new thematic tour, it may be time to part ways. Be clear and direct. Neither the site nor the guide benefits by prolonging this less than amicable arrangement.

❖ *Remember: respect the needs of individuals and the site. Be flexible, be creative, yet stay the course!*

Performance Standards for the Site

Performance standards are a two-way street. In a very real sense, the site and the guide are responsible to each other. While everyone tends to think about performance standards in terms of the guides, it is the site's responsibility to make it possible for the guide to do an excellent job of giving tours. In considering how to talk with guides about standards, make a list of performance standards for the site. For example, it is the site's responsibility to:

- Provide guides with an excellent training program
- Provide a helpful mentor to support the orientation process
- Give the guide a fair and reasonable schedule, with adequate time for breaks and advance notice if changes are necessary
- Respond to problems or questions in a timely manner
- Foster collegial peer relationships among all staff
- Provide opportunities for continued enrichment
- Provide an environment in which the guide can do her best

As part of the performance evaluation process, talk with guides about the site's responsibilities, perhaps asking them to generate such a list. The *Program Review* form that follows is a good way to get feedback about whether the site is fulfilling its responsibilities from the guides' perspectives.

Caleb Crawley House Program Review

SAMPLE

To: (guide)

From: (supervisor)

Date:

Please take a few minutes to provide some feedback that will contribute to evaluating the current success of our work and our workplace. Thank you.

I felt good about working at the *Caleb Crawley House* recently when . . .

I was disappointed/upset concerning my work at the *Caleb Crawley House* recently when . . .

What I like best about giving tours is . . .

If I could realistically change one thing about the tours or tour operation it would be . . .

The position of guide would be better if . . .

List any concerns you have relating to (insert name of program)

List any suggestions you have for improving our work/workplace

Performance Standards for Guides

Guides should be informed about the standards by which their performance will be measured at the annual review. One way to do this is to provide a list of standards that correspond to the measures cited on the *Annual Tour Review*. Another option is to provide guides with blank copies of the assessment form. A sample *Annual Tour Review* assessment form follows.

Caleb Crawley House Annual Tour Review

SAMPLE

Guide: ______________________________ Date: ____________________

Signed ______________________________ *Date* ____________________
guide

Signed ______________________________ *Date* ____________________
supervisor

Presentation of Content

How did the guide perform in the following areas relating to presentation of content?

Clear communication of the storyline and themes of the tour

Excellent Good Fair Needs Support

Selection of appropriate evidence to illustrate the themes

Excellent Good Fair Needs Support

Encouraging questions and taking time to answer them

Excellent Good Fair Needs Support

Presenting information concisely and giving time for visitors to experience the site through their senses

Excellent Good Fair Needs Support

Holding the interest of the group

Excellent Good Fair Needs Support

Accurately "reading" the audience and adapting the tour accordingly?

Excellent Good Fair Needs Support

Answering questions about the building and the people associated with it, the architecture, the furnishings, and the landscape

Excellent Good Fair Needs Support

In what area is the guide particularly strong in content?

In what area could the guide use more content support?

Procedures

How did the guide perform in the following areas relating to procedures?

Managing the group's movements and behavior appropriately

Excellent Good Fair Needs Support

Reminding visitors not to touch the walls or objects in the building

Excellent Good Fair Needs Support

Taking adequate and appropriate steps to ensure the safety of the collection

Excellent Good Fair Needs Support

Exhibiting flexibility and showing good judgment in dealing with unexpected situations

Excellent Good Fair Needs Support

Effectiveness at communicating and supporting site policies and procedures (photography, touching, group size, etc.)

Excellent Good Fair Needs Support

Informing visitors about the benefits of membership, encouraging them to join, and telling them about other program opportunities at the site

Excellent Good Fair Needs Support

Personal Characteristics

How did the guide perform in the following areas relating to personal characteristics?

Being welcoming and helpful to the visitors

Excellent Good Fair Needs Support

Pleasant and effective speech

Excellent Good Fair Needs Support

Neat grooming appropriate for working as an interpreter of a historic site

Excellent Good Fair Needs Support

Performing his/her job in a conscientious and professional manner

Excellent Good Fair Needs Support

Friendliness of body language

Excellent Good Fair Needs Support

Speaking and acting in the best interests of the site

Excellent Good Fair Needs Support

General

Rate the guide's progress since his/her last tour review

Excellent Good Fair Needs Support

What are the guide's strengths?

In what areas is more support needed?

Self-Evaluation

A self-evaluation that parallels the formal assessment (Form 8.8) can help guides focus and reflect upon their individual skills. Guides can be encouraged to do self-evaluations at any time, but may find it particularly useful in the month before the annual tour review. In many ways, a self-evaluation can serve as good practice for the more formal annual review. Given the self-evaluation's relative informality, guides may ask mentors for feedback if desired. Also, give the option of keeping these self-evaluations private.

FORM 8.9

Self-Evaluation Questionnaire

Presentation of Content

____ Did I clearly communicate the storyline and themes of the tour?

____ Did I select appropriate evidence to illustrate the themes?

____ Did I encourage questions and take the time to answer them?

____ Did I present the information concisely and give time for visitors to experience the site through their senses?

____ Did I hold the interest of the group?

____ Did I accurately "read" my audience and adapt the tour accordingly?

____ Was I able to answer questions about the building and the people associated with it? About the architecture? The furnishings? The landscape?

Procedures

____ Did I manage the group's movements and behavior appropriately?

____ Did I remind visitors not to touch the walls and the objects in the building?

____ Did I take adequate and appropriate steps to insure the safety of the collection?

____ Did I exhibit flexibility and show good judgment in dealing with unexpected situations?

____ Did I effectively communicate and support site policies and procedures? (photography, touching, group size, etc.)

____ Did I inform visitors of the benefits of membership, encourage them to join, and tell them about other program opportunities at the site?

Personal Characteristics

____ Was I welcoming and helpful to visitors?

____ Was my speech pleasant to listen to and effective?

____ Was I neatly groomed for working as an interpreter of a historic site?

____ Did I perform my job in a conscientious and professional manner?

____ Did I speak and act in the best interests of the site?

____ Did I employ friendly body language?

Bibliography

This bibliography is intended to provide relevant background and informational readings that are both practical and for the most part readily available. We have chosen to start with a list of selected books and articles that have most influenced our work. These are followed by a broader list organized topically. Generally, we have chosen to include books and articles published in the last twenty years or so, as these are often easiest to find. However, some older books and journal articles are excellent sources for helpful information, and we recommend that those with a serious interest pursue these as well. A source list of professional journals and technical leaflets follows this bibliography.

SELECTED LIST

Butcher-Younghans, Sherry. *Historic House Museums: A Practical Handbook for Their Care, Preservation, and Management.* New York: Oxford University Press, 1993.

Carson, Barbara G. "Interpreting History Through Objects," *Roundtable Reports* 10, no. 3 (1984): 2–5.

Carson, Cary, and Barbara G. Carson. "Things Unspoken: Learning Social History from Artifacts." In *Ordinary People and Everyday Life: Perspectives on the New Social History,* ed. James B. Gardener and George Rollie Adams, 181–203. Nashville, Tenn.: American Association for State and Local History, 1985.

Diamond, Judy. *Practical Evaluation Guide: Tools for Museums and Other Informal Education Settings.* Walnut Creek, Calif.: AltaMira, 1999.

Falk, John H., and Lynn D. Dierking. *The Museum Experience.* Washington, D.C.: Whalesback, 1992.

Grinder, Alison L., and E. Sue McCoy. *The Good Guide: A Sourcebook for Interpreters, Docents and Tour Guides.* Scottsdale, Ariz.: Ironwood, 1985.

Ham, Sam H. *Environmental Interpretation: A Practical Guide for People with Big Ideas and Small Budgets.* Golden, Colo.: Fulcrum, 1992.

Hein, George E. *Learning in the Museum.* New York: Routledge, 1998.

Schlereth, Thomas J. "Object Knowledge: Every Museum Visitor an Interpreter," *Roundtable Reports* 9, no. 1 (1984): 5–9.

Tilden, Freeman. *Interpreting Our Heritage.* 3d ed. Chapel Hill: University of North Carolina Press, 1977.

Woods, Thomas A. "Perspectivistic Interpretation: A New Direction for Sites and Exhibits," *History News* 44, no. 1 (1989): 14, 27–28.

GENERAL MUSEUM

Alexander, Edward P. *Museums in Motion: An Introduction to the History and Function of Museums.* Walnut Creek, Calif.: AltaMira, 1996.

Ambrose, Timothy, and Crispin Paine. *Museum Basics.* New York: Routledge, 1993.

American Association of Museums. *Code of Ethics for Museums.* Washington, D.C.: American Association of Museums, 2000.

American Association of Museums, Historic Sites Committee. *An Annotated Bibliography for the Development and Operations of Historic Sites.* Washington, D.C.: American Association of Museums, 1982.

Burcaw, G. Ellis. *Introduction to Museum Work.* 3d ed. Walnut Creek, Calif.: AltaMira, 1997.

Butcher-Younghans, Sherry. *Historic House Museums: A Practical Handbook for Their Care, Preservation and Management.* New York: Oxford University Press, 1993.

Falk, John H., and Lynn D. Dierking. *The Museum Experience.* Washington, D.C.: Whalesback, 1992.

Leon, Warren, and Roy Rosenzweig. *History Museums in the United States: A Critical Assessment.* Urbana: University of Illinois Press, 1989.

Miller, Ronald L. *Personnel Policies for Museums: A Handbook for Management.* Washington, D.C.: American Association of Museums, 1980.

Rosenzweig, Roy, and David Thelen. *The Presence of the Past: Popular Uses of History in American Life.* New York: Columbia University Press, 1998.

Skramstad, Harold. "An Agenda for American Museums in the Twenty-First Century," *Daedalus* 128, no. 3 (1999): 109–28.

Walker, Patricia Chambers, and Thomas Graham, comps. *Directory of Historic House Museums in the United States.* Walnut Creek, Calif.: AltaMira, 1999.

Wallace, Michael. "Visiting the Past: History Museums in the United States," *Radical History Review* 25 (1981).

INTERPRETATION AND GUIDE TRAINING

Alderson, William T., and Shirley Payne Low. *Interpretation of Historic Sites.* 2d ed., rev. Walnut Creek, Calif.: AltaMira, 1985.

Anderson, Jay. *A Living History Reader.* Nashville, Tenn.: American Association for State and Local History, 1991; distributed by AltaMira.

Anderson, Jay. *The Living History Sourcebook.* Nashville, Tenn.: American Association for State and Local History, 1985.

Anderson, Jay. *Time Machines: The World of Living History.* Nashville, Tenn.: American Association for State and Local History, 1984.

Beck, Larry, and Ted Cable. *Interpretation for the 21st Century.* Champaign, Ill.: Sagamore, 1998.

Blatti, Jo, ed. *Past Meets Present: Essays About Historic Interpretation and Public Audiences.* Washington, D.C.: Smithsonian Institution Press, 1987.

Booth, J. H., G. H. Krockover, and P. R. Woods. *Creative Museum Methods and Educational Techniques.* Springfield, Ill.: Charles C. Thomas, 1982.

Edson, Gary. "The Quandaries of Museum Training," *Journal of Museum Education* 20, no. 1 (1995): 12–14.

Gillette, Jane Brown. "Breaking the Silence," *Historic Preservation*, 47, no. 2 (1995): 38–43.

Glassberg, David. "Presenting History to the Public: The Study of Memory and the Uses of the Past," *CRM* 21, no. 11 (1998): 4–8.

Grinder, Alison L., and E. Sue McCoy. *The Good Guide: A Sourcebook for Interpreters, Docents and Tour Guides.* Scottsdale, Ariz.: Ironwood, 1985.

Ham, Sam H. "Cognitive Psychology and Interpretation: Synthesis and Application," *Journal of Interpretation* 8, no. 1 (1983): 11–27.

———. *Environmental Interpretation: A Practical Guide for People with Big Ideas and Small Budgets.* Golden, Colo.: Fulcrum, 1992.

Horn, A. "The Adult Tour Dilemma," *Roundtable Reports* 4, no. 4 (1979): 1–4.

Krockover, Gerald H., and Jeanette Hauck. *Training for Docents: How to Talk to Visitors.* Technical Leaflet, no. 125. Nashville, Tenn.: American Association for State and Local History, 1980.

Lessinger, L., and D. Gillis. *Teaching As a Performing Art.* Dallas: Crescendo, 1976.

Levy, Barbara A., and Susan P. Schreiber. "The View From the Kitchen," *History News* 50, no. 2 (1995): 16–20.

Lewis, William J. *Interpreting for Park Visitors.* Philadelphia: Eastern Acorn, 1981.

Machlis, Gary E., and Donald R. Field. *On Interpretation: Sociology for Interpreters of Natural and Cultural History.* Rev. ed. Corvallis: Oregon State University Press, 1992.

Marsh, C. "How to Encourage Museum Visitors to Ask Questions: An Experimental Investigation," *Roundtable Reports* 8, no. 2 (1983): 18–19.

McKay, Jim. "Interpreting Servants at the Martin Van Buren NHS," *CRM* 20, no. 3 (1997): 48.

Parsons, Chris. "Starting an Interpreter Evaluation Program," *Legacy* 7 (1996): 8–12.

Regnier, Kathleen, Michael Gross, and Ron Zimmerman. *The Interpreter's Guide Book: Techniques for Programs and Presentations.* 3d ed. Interpreter's Handbook Series. Stevens Point, Wisc.: UW-SP Foundation Press, 1994.

Row, James, Mary Weiland, and Brad Thiel. "Stepping into the Other Person's Shoes: Interpreting Conflict from Multiple Perspectives," *History News* 53, no. 2 (1998): 7–11.

Schreiber, Susan P. "Interpreting Slavery at National Trust Sites: A Case Study in Addressing Difficult Topics," *CRM* 23, no. 5 (2000): 49–52.

Schroeder, Fred E. H. *Interpreting and Reinterpreting Associative Historic Sites and Artifacts.* Technical Report, no. 6. Nashville, Tenn.: American Association for State and Local History, 1986.

Spude, Robert L. "Exploring Hispanic History and Culture," *CRM* 20, no. 11 (1997): 6–7.

Tilden, Freeman. *Interpreting Our Heritage.* 3d ed. Chapel Hill: University of North Carolina Press, 1977.

Vlach, John Michael. "Confronting Slavery: One Example of the Perils and Promise of Difficult History," *History News* 54, no. 2 (1999): 12–15.

West, Patricia. "Interpreting Women's History at Male-Focused House Museums," *CRM* 20, no. 3 (1997): 8–9.

Williams, Wayne E., and Edward N. Schultz. "Dealing with the Disturbing: Interpreting Pain and Suffering," *Legacy* (1996): 28–30.

Wolins, Inez S. "Teaching the Teachers: This Approach to Docent Education Wisely Acknowledges That the People Who Lead Museum Tours Are Learners as Well as Teachers," *Museum News* 69, no. 3 (1990): 71–75.

MATERIAL CULTURE

Beck, T. R., P. K. Eversmann, R. T. Krill, R. Michael, and B. A. Twiss-Garrity. "Material Culture as Text: Review and Reform of the Literacy Model for Interpretation." In *Material Culture: The Shape of the Field. Proceedings of the 1992 Winterthur Conference,* 135–67. Winterthur, Del.: Henry Francis Dupont Winterthur Museum, 1997.

Carson, Barbara G. "Interpreting History Through Objects," *Roundtable Reports* 10, no. 3 (1984): 2–5.

Carson, Cary, and Barbara G. Carson. "Things Unspoken: Learning Social History from Artifacts." In *Ordinary People and Everyday Life: Perspectives on the New Social History*, ed. James B. Gardener and George Rollie Adams, 181–203. Nashville, Tenn.: American Association for State and Local History, 1983.

Durbin, Gail, Susan Morris, and Sue Wilkinson. *Learning From Objects.* London: English Heritage, 1996.

Krill, Rosemary Troy, with Pauline K. Eversmann. *Early American Decorative Arts, 1620–1860: A Handbook for Interpreters.* Walnut Creek, Calif.: AltaMira in association with Winterthur Museum Gardens and Library, 2001.

Lloyd, Sandra Mackenzie. "Giving Objects Their Voice," *Minds in Motion: The Docent Educator* 4, no. 3 (1995): 14–16.

Lubar, Steve, and W. David Kingery, eds. *History from Things: Essays on Material Culture.* Washington, D.C.: Smithsonian Institution Press, 1993.

Pearce, Susan M., ed. *Museum Studies in Material Culture.* Washington, D.C.: Smithsonian Institution Press, 1989.

Schlereth, Thomas J. *Artifacts and the American Past,* Walnut Creek, Calif.: AltaMira, 1980.

———, ed. *Material Culture Studies in America: An Anthology.* Walnut Creek, Calif.: AltaMira, 1999.

———. "Object Knowledge: Every Museum Visitor an Interpreter," *Roundtable Reports* 9, no. 1 (1984): 5–9.

Woods, Thomas A. "Perspectivistic Interpretation: A New Direction for Sites and Exhibits," *History News* 44, no. 1 (1989): 14, 27–28.

AUDIENCE

American Association of Museums. *The Accessible Museum: Model Programs of Accessibility for Disabled and Older People*. Washington, D.C.: American Association of Museums, 1993.

American Association of Museums. *Excellence and Equity: Education and the Public Dimension of Museums*. Washington, D.C.: American Association of Museums, 1992.

Chambers, Marlene, "What Research Says Beyond 'Aha!': Motivating Museum Visitors," *ILVS Review* 1, no. 2 (1990).

Cornell Cooperative Extension. *Resources for Parents and Others Who Care about Children*. Ithaca, N.Y.: Cornell University, 1982.

Dierking, Lynn D., "The Family Museum Experience: Implications from Research," *Journal of Museum Education* 14, no. 2 (spring/summer 1989).

Falk, John H. "A Framework for Diversifying Museum Audiences: Putting Heart and Head in the Right Place," *Museum News* 77, no. 5 (1998): 36–39, 61.

———. *Leisure Decisions Influencing African American Use of Museums*. Washington, D.C.: American Association of Museums, 1991.

———. "Visitors: Who Does, Who Doesn't, and Why," *Museum News* 77, no. 2 (1998): 38–42.

Falk, John H., and Lynn D. Dierking. "Assessing the Long-Term Impact of School Field Trips," *Current Trends in Audience Research and Evaluation* 8 (1994): 71–74.

Finn, David. *How to Visit a Museum*. New York: Harry Abrams, 1985.

Groff, Gerda, and Laura Gardner. *What Museum Guides Need to Know: Access for Blind and Visually Impaired Visitors*. New York: American Foundation for the Blind, 1989.

Hilke, D. D. "Strategies for Family Learning in Museums." In *Visitor Studies: Theory, Research, and Practice,* eds. S. Bitgood, J. T. Roper Jr., and A Benefield, 121–34. Jacksonville, Fla.: Center for Social Design, 1988.

Hood, M. G. "After 70 Years of Audience Research, What Have We Learned? Who Comes to Museums, Who Does Not, and Why?" In *Visitor Studies: Theory, Research, and Practice*, vol. 5, ed. D. Thompson et al., 16–27. Jacksonville, Fla.: Visitor Studies Association, 1993.

Hooper-Greenhill, Eilean. *Museums and Their Visitors*. New York: Routledge, 1994.

Joffee, Elga, and Mary Ann Siller. *Reaching Out: A Creative Access Guide for Designing Exhibits and Cultural Programs for Persons Who Are Blind or Visually Impaired*. New York: American Foundation for the Blind, 1998.

Kenney, Alice P. *Access to the Past: Museum Programs and Handicapped Visitors*. Nashville, Tenn.: American Association for State and Local History, 1982.

Majewski, Janice. *Part of Your General Public Is Disabled*. Washington, D.C.: Smithsonian Institution Press, 1987.

National Park Service, Special Programs and Populations Branch. *Interpretation for Disabled Visitors in the National Park System*. Washington, D.C.: National Park Service, n.d.

Robertson, Susan, and Lana Lewis. "New Audiences: Breaking Down Invisible Barriers," *History News* 51, no. 2 (1996): 10–12.

Salmen, John P. S., ed. *Everyone's Welcome: The Americans with Disabilities Act and Museums*. Washington, D.C.: American Association for Museums, 1998.

United States Architectural and Transportation Barriers Compliance Board. *Americans with Disabilities Act: Accessibility Guidelines for Buildings and Facilities*. Washington, D.C.: Government Printing Office, 1991.

EDUCATION AND LEARNING

Baldwin, Luke, Sharlene Cochrane, Constance Counts, Joan Dolamore, Martha McKenna, and Barbara Vacarr. "Passionate and Purposeful: Adult Learning Communities," *Journal of Museum Education* 15, no. 1 (1990): 7–9. Also, reprinted in *Patterns in Practice: Selections from the Journal of Museum Education*, 162–67. Washington D.C.: Museum Education Roundtable, 1992.

Bateman, Walter L. *Open to Question: The Art of Teaching and Learning by Inquiry*. San Francisco: Jossey-Bass, 1990.

Booth, Jeanette Hauck, et al. *Creative Museum Methods and Educational Techniques*. Springfield, Ill.: Clarence C. Thomas, 1982.

Byrne, Karen. "The Power of Place: Using Historic Structures to Teach Children about Slavery," *CRM* 23, no. 3 (2000): 9–10.

Cherry, Florence J. *Ages and Stages of the Middle-Years Child, Part I: Six- to Eight-Year-Olds*. Ithaca, N.Y.: Cornell Cooperative Extension, 1991.

Cherry, Florence J. *Ages and Stages of the Middle-Years Child, Part II: Nine- to Eleven-Year-Olds*. Ithaca, N.Y.: Cornell Cooperative Extension, 1995.

Csikszentmihalyi, Mihaly, and Kim Hermanson. "Intrinsic Motivation in Museums: What Makes Visitors Want to Learn?" *Museum News* 74, no. 3 (1995): 34–37, 59–62.

Davis, Jessica, and Howard Gardner. "Open Windows, Open Doors," *Museum News* 72, no. 1 (1993): 34–37, 57–58.

Dierking, Lynn D. "Learning Theory and Learning Styles: An Overview," *Journal of Museum Education* 16, no. 1 (winter 1991).

Duckworth, E. "Museum Visitors and the Development of Understanding," *Journal of Museum Education* 15, no. 1 (winter 1990): 4–6.

Falk, John H., and Lynn D. Dierking. *Learning from Museums: Visitor Experiences and the Making of Meaning*. Walnut Creek, Calif.: AltaMira, 2000.

Fosnot, C. T., ed. *Constructivism: Theory, Perspectives, and Practice.* New York: Teachers College Press, 1996.

Gardner, Howard. *Frames of Mind: The Theory of Multiple Intelligences.* New York: Basic, 1985.

Gartenhaus, Alan. *Minds in Motion: Using Museums to Expand Creative Thinking.* Davis, Calif.: Caddo Gap, 1991.

Gartenhaus, Alan, and Jackie Littleton, eds. *The Best of the Docent Educator: A Comprehensive Manual for Those Who Teach with Institutional Collections.* Kamuela, Hawaii: Docent Educator, 1998.

Hamilton, Stephen F. *Adolescents.* Ithaca, N.Y.: Cornell Cooperative Extension, 1988.

Hein, George E. "How Children Behave in Museums," *ICOM Education* 12–13 (1991): 52–57.

———. *Learning in the Museum.* New York: Routledge, 1998.

Hein, George E., and Mary Alexander. *Museums: Places of Learning.* Professional Practice series. Washington, D.C.: American Association of Museums, 1998.

Henderson, Anne, and Susy Watts. "Learning How They Learn: The Family in the Museum," *Museum News* 79, no. 6 (2000): 40–45, 67.

Henry, Barbara. "Questioning Strategies: For Adults Only," *Docent Educator* 1, no. 1 (autumn 1991): 6–7.

Hirsch, Joanne S., and Lois H. Silverman, eds. *Transforming Practice: Selections from the Journal of Museum Education, 1992–1999.* Washington, D.C.: Museum Education Roundtable, 2000.

Hooper-Greenhill, Eilean. *Museums and the Shaping of Knowledge.* New York: Routledge, 1991.

Horton, James Oliver. "On-Site Learning: The Power of Historic Places," *CRM* 23, no. 8 (2000): 4–5.

Kaufmann, Felice. "Reappraising Praise: Responding to Visitors' Answers," *Docent Educator* 1, no. 3 (spring 1992): 6–7.

Littleton, Jackie. "Inquiry and the Primary Learner: Questions and Young Children," *Docent Educator* 1, no. 3 (spring 1992): 4–5.

Merrian, S. B., and R. S. Caffarella. *Learning in Adulthood: A Comprehensive Guide.* San Francisco: Jossey-Bass, 1991.

Miller, George. "The Magical Number Seven, Plus or Minus Two: Some Limits on Our Capacity for Processing Information," *Psychological Review* 63, no. 2 (1956): 81–97.

National Park Service. *Programming for School Groups: An Interpreter's Guide.* Washington, D.C.: National Park Service, 1991.

Norman, Donald A. *Learning and Memory.* New York: W. H. Freeman, 1982.

O'Connell, Peter. "Adult Education and the Museum Experience," *History News* 43, no.5 (September/October 1988): 10–17.

Pitman, Bonnie, ed. *Presence of Mind: Museums and the Spirit of Learning.* Washington, D.C.: American Association of Museums, 1999.

Roberts, L. *From Knowledge to Narrative: Educators and the Changing Museum.* Washington, D.C.: Smithsonian Institution Press, 1997.

Schmeck, R. R. *Learning Strategies and Learning Styles.* New York: Plenum, 1987.

Shepperd, Beverly, ed. *Building Museum and School Partnerships.* Washington, D.C.: American Association of Museums with the Pennsylvania Federation of Museums and Historical Organizations, 1993.

Shoemaker, Marla K. "Watching Children Grow: A Guide to Childhood Development," *Docent Educator* 2, no. 1 (autumn 1992).

Vukelich, R. "Time Language for Interpreting History Collections to Children," *Museum Studies Journal* 1, no. 4 (1984): 43–50.

EVALUATION

American Association of Museums, Committee on Audience Research and Evaluation. *Introduction to Museum Evaluation.* Resource Report. Washington, D.C.: American Association of Museums, 1999.

Bitgood, Stephen, and Harris H. Shettel. "An Overview of Visitor Studies," *Journal of Museum Education* 21, no. 3 (1996): 6–10.

Brady, John. *The Craft of Interviewing.* New York: Random House, 1977.

Chen, Huey-tsyh, *Theory-Driven Evaluations.* Newbury Park, Calif.: Sage Publications, 1990.

Covert, R. W. *Guidelines and Criteria for Constructing Questionnaires.* Charlottesville: University of Virginia, Evaluation Research Center, 1977.

Diamond, Judy. *Practical Evaluation Guide: Tools for Museums and Other Informal Education Settings.* Walnut Creek, Calif.: AltaMira, 1999.

Fink, A. and J. Kosecoff. *How to Conduct Surveys: A Step-by-Step Guide.* Newbury Park, Calif.: Sage Publications, 1987.

Freeman, H. E., G. D. Sandfur, and P. H. Rossi. *Workbook for Evaluation: A Systematic Approach.* Newbury Park, Calif.: Sage Publications, 1989.

Frey, J. *Survey Research by Telephone*, 2d ed. Newbury Park, Calif.: Sage Publications, 1983.

Furano, Kathryn, Linda Z. Jucovy, David P. Racine, and Thomas J. Smith. *The Essential Connection: Using Evaluation to Identify Programs Worth Replicating.* Philadelphia: Replication and Program Strategies, 1995.

Guba, E. C., and Y. S. Lincoln. *Effective Evaluation.* San Francisco: Jossey-Bass, 1981.

Herman, J. L. *Program Evaluation Kit.* 2d ed. Newbury Park, Calif.: Sage Publications, 1990.

Korn, Randi, and Laurie Sowd. *Visitor Surveys: A User's Manual.* Resource Report. Washington, D.C.: American Association of Museums, 1990.

Kosecoff, Jacqueline, and Arlene Fink. *Evaluation Basics: A Practitioner's Manual.* Newbury Park, Calif.: Sage Publications, 1982.

Krueger, R. A. *Focus Groups: A Practical Guide for Applied Research.* Newbury Park, Calif.: Sage Publications, 1988.

Patton, Michael Quinn. *Practical Evaluation.* Newbury Park, Calif.: Sage Publications, 1982.

Rossi, Pete H., and Howard E. Freeman. *Evaluation: A Systematic Approach.* Newbury Park, Calif.: Sage Publications, 1993.

Runyard, S. *Low Cost Visitor Surveys: Guidance on Market Research for Small and Medium Sized Museums.* London: Museums and Galleries Association, 1994.

Taylor, Samuel, ed. *Try It! Improving Exhibits Through Formative Evaluation.* Washington, D.C.: American Association of Museums, 1992.

W. K. Kellogg Foundation Evaluation Handbook. Battle Creek, Mich.: Kellogg Foundation, 1998.

Wholey, Joseph S., Harry P. Hatry, and Kathryn E. Newcomer, eds. *Handbook of Practical Program Evaluation.* San Francisco: Jossey-Bass, 1994.

Wilson, Marlene. *The Effective Management of Volunteer Programs.* Washington, D.C.: American Association of Museums, 1976.

PROFESSIONAL ORGANIZATIONS, JOURNALS, MAGAZINES, AND TECHNICAL LEAFLETS

ALHFAM Bulletin
ALHFAM Proceedings
Association for Living History, Farm and Agricultural Museums
8774 Route 45NW
North Bloomfield, OH 44450
(440) 685-4410
www.alhfam.org

American Historical Review
American Historical Association
400 A Street, SE
Washington, DC 20003
(202) 544-2422
www.theaha.org

CRM (Cultural Resource Management)
National Center for Cultural Resources
National Park Service
1849 C Street, NW, NC-350
Washington, DC 20240
(202) 343-3411
www.cr.nps.gov/crm

History Matters
National Council for History Education
26915 Westlake Road, Suite B-2
Westlake, OH 44145
(440) 835-1776
www.history.org/nche/

History News
History News Technical Leaflet
American Association for State and Local History
1717 Church Street
Nashville, TN 37203
(615) 320-3203
www.aaslh.org

Journal of American History
OAH Magazine of History
Organization of American Historians
112 North Bryan Avenue
Bloomington, IN 47408
(812) 855-7311
www.oah.org

Journal of Interpretation Research
Legacy
National Association for Interpretation
P.O. Box 2246
Fort Collins, CO 80522
(888) 900-8283
www.interpnet.com or www.interpnet.org

Journal of Museum Education
Museum Education Roundtable
621 Pennsylvania Avenue, SE
Washington, DC 20003
(202) 547-8378
www.mer-online.org

Museum News
American Association of Museums
1575 Eye Street, NW, Suite 400
Washington, DC 20005
(202) 289-1818
www.aam-us.org

Preservation
National Trust for Historic Preservation
1785 Massachusetts Avenue, NW
Washington, DC 20036
(202) 588-6000
www.nthp.org

The Public Historian
National Council on Public History
327 Cavanaugh Hall–IUPUI
425 University Boulevard CA327
Indianapolis, IN 46202
(317) 274-2716
www.ncph.org

Social Education
National Council for the Social Studies
8555 Sixteenth St., Ste. 500
Silver Spring, MD 20910
(301) 588-1800
www.ncss.org

Visitor Studies Today!
Visitor Studies Association
P.O. Box 470845
Aurora, CO 80047
(303) 337-4301
www.museum.msu.edu/vsa/

About the Authors

Barbara Abramoff Levy first practiced her interpretation skills as a choral conductor, singer, and music teacher. Although she moved on to work in the historic site field, her experiences in music and teaching confirmed her belief that interpretation in any field required understanding and effective communication. Her professional commitment to creating great interpretive experiences at historic sites began when she was the Interpretation Planner for the Massachusetts Department of Environmental Management, Planning Division, and continued when she became Director of Education and Interpretation for the Society for the Preservation of New England Antiquities. In 1993 she founded Barbara Levy Associates, a consulting group that has helped history museums and historical organizations across the country improve their interpretation, planning, and education programs. Well known as a skilled interpretive planner, teacher, and trainer, she is also a frequently requested presenter at regional and national professional conferences. She holds a bachelor of music degree (with distinction) from the University of Michigan, and both master of music and master of arts degrees from Boston University.

Sandy Mackenzie Lloyd first interpreted history to the public as a kindergartner, when she wrote, directed, and starred in a play about Betsy Ross. A year later she began collecting antiques, and she was hooked. Her combined love of history and "things" led to degrees in American studies from Smith College and early American culture from the Winterthur Program at the University of Delaware. She was the first curator of Wyck, a historic house in Philadelphia, and the Curator of Education at Cliveden, a property of the National Trust for Historic Preservation. She has written several historic structures reports for significant buildings in Philadelphia, given tours of historic sites for over twenty years, conducted guide training, lectured, and taught the toughest historic site audience—schoolchildren. She lives with her family in Philadelphia, where she works as a museum consultant to many historic sites, including Pennsbury Manor, Paulsdale, Montpelier, the Woodrow Wilson House, Washington's Crossing, and the Betsy Ross House.

Susan Porter Schreiber began her career teaching seventh through twelfth grades on the outskirts of a Connecticut thread mill town, learning from students about their dreams and their needs for a sense of connection to the larger world. She cut her teeth in museum education, working with schoolchildren and training guides in the early 1970s at Old Sturbridge Village, a hotbed of ideas about work, family, and community in the past and how museums could make a difference in our society. She was a Rockefeller Foundation Fellow in Museum Education at the Metropolitan Museum of Art and worked on a variety of curriculum development, exhibition, and historic site projects. In 1979, she moved to Washington, D.C., to serve as a program officer at the National Endowment for the Humanities, and she subsequently served as Assistant Director of the American Association of Museums. From 1988 to 2000 she was Director of Interpretation and Education for the National Trust for Historic Preservation. She is currently Vice President for Public Programs for the Historical Society of Washington, D.C., where she is working on the creation of the City Museum. Susan has a bachelor of arts degree from Duke University and a master's degree in English and education from the University of Connecticut.

Index

architect, 8
architectural historian, 8, 13
archives, 8, 64
articulation, 120
assessment; performance, 139; self-evaluation, 147–148
audience; adapting site message to, 109–110; age of, 111, 112; identifying, 9; special needs, 113; *See also* visitor
autistic gesture, 122–123

bibliography, for notebook, 9
biography; Benjamin Crawley, fictional biography of, 55–56; Caleb Crawley, fictional biography of, 54; Elizabeth Budd Crawley, fictional biography of, 54–55; fictional (sample), 54–65; goal of, 93; historical, 7–8, 23, 26, 27, 28, 54, 87, 92; in thematic tour outline, 38, 40, 43
board of directors, 12
brainstorming, 11, 12, 14 (box), 29, 40, 110
breathing technique, 119
buildings, interpretation of, 74

Caleb Crawley House, 127; annual tour review (sample), 144–146; background material for, 10 (box); biographies for, 54–56; guide agreement (sample), 134; guide application (sample), 132; guide duty (sample), 129; interpretive commentary (sample), 43; roundtable workshop for, 15–19; site topic of, 29–30; storyline of, 23; theme of, 23–24, 31–33, 43; time line for, 52–53
CAP. *See* Conservation Assessment Program
Chinese export teacup, interpreting, 74–75
class, social, 6
collection objects, 8. *See also* material culture
communication, goal of, 101. *See also* communication training; communication training activity
communication skill, tip for, 108
communication training; preparation for, 82; strategy for, 82–83; *See also* communication; communication training activity
communication training activity; adapting site message to audience, 109–110; becoming the audience, 103–104, 105; gesture use, 122–123; interpreting sensitive topics, 114–115, 116, 117; special needs audience, 113; understanding communication process, 106–107; voice use, 118–121; working with age groups, 111, 112; *See also* communication; communication training
conservation, 3
Conservation Assessment Program (CAP), 8
consultant, 12–13
curator, 12, 13, 64, 68

emphatic gesture, 122
exhibitions, 4 (box)
expression, in speech, 120–121

focus group, 9
fictional biographies; Benjamin Crawley, 55–56; Caleb Crawley, 54; Elizabeth Budd Crawley, 54–55
furnishing plan, period room, 8

gender, 6
gesture; autistic, 122–123; emphatic, 122; illustrative, 122; indicative, 122; *Good Guide* (Grinder and McCoy), 112; grant proposals, 8; grants for planning, 12; guest log, 9; guide, hiring; advertising/recruitment, 130; application (sample), 132; guide agreement, 133, 134; guide duty, 128, 129; interviewing, 133; orientation, 133; planning for, 128; position qualification, 130; *See also* guide, management of
guide, management of, 127–128; advisory committee for, 127–128; annual tour review (sample), 144–146; guide training checklist, 135, 136; guides who resist change, 140; mentor checklist for, 138; mentor/trainee agreement for, 137; mentoring program, 135; paying guides, 131; performance assessment, 139; program review (sample), 142; self-evaluation, by guide, 147, 148; volunteer, 127, 131; *See also* guide, hiring
guide training, 3, 8, 59; core information for, 61; curriculum, 59–60; goal of, 61; guide training checklist, 135, 136; preparation for, 59–60; strategy for, 61–62; tips for, 112; *See also* communication training; guide training, site specifics; guide,

management of; material culture training; thematic tour training
guide training, site specifics; enrichment activity, 64–65; lecture/tour for, 63; readings about site, 62; site/collection familiarization, 63–64; welcome, 62
guided tour, xi–xii, 3, 12; focus of, xii; *See also* thematic tour

historic house setting, 26
historic landscape report (HLR), 8
historic object. *See* material culture
historic site; identifying topics for, 29–30; mission of, 3; options for interpretation, 4 (box); resources of, 3–4; thematic interpretation of, 7, 27
historic structure report (HSR), 8
historical biography, 7–8, 23, 26, 54, 87, 92–93
historical context; definition of, 25, 81, 87; example of, 25; interpreting individual space, 41, 42; material culture training activity, 78, 79, 80; thematic tour training activity, 89, 96; training goal of, 61; training strategy for, 23, 25, 38, 40, 43, 61–62
historical landscape report (HLR), 8
history, definition of, 24
HLR. *See* historic landscape report
HSR. *See* historic structure report
human learning stages, 112

illustrative gesture, 122
IMLS. *See* Institute for Museum and Library Services
indicative gesture, 122
Institute for Museum and Library Services (IMLS), 8
interpretation, 59; of controversial topic, 6; multidimensional, 6; organizing element of, 23; what it is not, 82; *See also* thematic tour; theme; theme development team
Interpreting Our Heritage (Tilden), 6
interpretive commentary (sample), 43

key idea. *See* theme

landscape architect, 8
library, on-site, 9

MAP. *See* Museum Assessment Program
market research, 9
material culture, 8; building interpretive tour with, 80; definition of, 69; evidence of, 96; example of, 69; in historic house setting, 26; structure of, 74; *See also* material culture training; material culture training activity
material culture/biography worksheet, 27
material culture/biography, use in interpretive tour, 26, 27, 28
material culture training, 67–68; goal of, 67; preparation for, 67–68; strategy for, 68; *See also* material culture; material culture training activity
material culture training activity; incorporating historical context, 78, 79, 80; interpreting material culture, 71–72, 73–76, 78; reading artifact, 77; reading physical evidence, 73–76; understanding material culture, 69–70; *See also* material culture; material culture training
mentor checklist (sample), 138; mentor, for guide in training, 12, 49 (box), 60, 61, 62, 135
mentor/trainee agreement (sample), 137
military history, 24
mission statement, 7
multiple perspectives; example of, 94; interpretation of, 94, 95
Museum Assessment Program (MAP), 8

National Endowment for the Humanities (NEH), 8
National Park Service, 3
NEH. *See* National Endowment for the Humanities
non-thematic tour, 86
notebook; biography for, 23; material for, 7–9

on-site library, 9
outline, thematic tour. *See* thematic tour outline

performance standards, guide, 139, 143
phonation, 119–120
physical evidence; collection objects (*see* material culture); definition of, 23, 24, 81, 87; thematic tour activity, 96, 97
planning grants, 12
portrait, interpreting, 75–76
Practical Evaluation Guide (Diamond), 50
preparation, notebook for, 7–9
presentation technique, 101–102
preservation, of collection, 3
primary source document, 64
project coordinator, 12, 14 (box)
public education, 3
public service coordinator, 12

race, 6
Rachel Jones, fictional biography of, 56
research; market, 9; unpublished, 9

research project, for training, 65
resonance, 119–120
room book, 8, 63–64
room card, 8, 63–64
room study, 63
roundtable workshop, 7, 37, 38; budget line item (sample), 15–16; for Caleb Crawley House, 15, 18, 19; checklist for, 14; component of, 11; goal of, 17; identifying storyline during, 17, 22; schedule (sample), 18, 19; staff members for, 12; *See also* roundtable workshop, steps in
roundtable workshop activity; identifying site theme, 31–33, 34–35; identifying site topic, 29–30; identifying storyline, 22, 23–25; understanding material culture, 26, 27, 28
roundtable workshop, steps in; establishing schedule, 14 (box); identifying team, 12–13; site staff preparation, 11–12; *See also* roundtable workshop

security, 3
self-evaluation, by guide, 147, 148
self-guided tour, 3, 4 (box)
sensitive topics; example of, 29, 116; guide tips for, 116, 117; training activity for, 114–115, 116, 117
site brochure, 7
site history, 7
site-specific training; goal of, 61; strategy for, 61–62
site topic; definition of, 29, 90; identifying, 29–30, 90
station tours, 3 (box)
stationed guide, 3 (box)
storage area, 64
storyline, 4; Caleb Crawley House, 23; definition of, 22, 23, 82, 87, 88; identifying, 17, 22, 23–25, 26; *See also* thematic tour outline

temporary guide, 49
thematic tour; component of, 2, 87, 88, 89, 90, 91, 92–93; definition of, 81; difference from non-thematic tour, 86; field assignment for, 103–104, 105; ideal number of theme for, 4, 81; preparation for, 7–9; teaching strategy for, 4; *See also* thematic tour outline; thematic tour training
thematic tour outline, 11, 98–99; component of, 37; drafting, 38, 39; final draft of, 48; organization of, 82; testing/revising, 38, 49–50; *See also* thematic tour; thematic tour training
thematic tour outline activity; creating rough outline, 41–42, 43, 44; interpreting individual space, 41–42, 43; refining outline, 47–48; revising outline, 49–50; revising storyline, 40; testing outline, 45–46, 49–50;
thematic tour training; goal of, 81–82; preparation for, 82–83; *See also* thematic tour; thematic tour outline; thematic tour training activity
thematic tour training activity; identifying site theme, 91; identifying site topic, 90; interpreting historical biography, 92–93, 94, 95; interpreting historical context, 89, 96; interpreting storyline, 88; practice, 99; thematic/non-thematic tour difference, 86; thematic tour component, 87; using evidence for interpretation, 96, 97
theme; of Caleb Crawley House, 23–24, 31–33, 34–35, 43; definition of, 23, 70, 81, 82, 87, 91; developing, 7, 11, 23–24, 31, 43, 81; identifying, 31–33, 34–35, 38, 40, 91; key topic in, 7, 29
theme building worksheet, 34–35
theme development team, 7, 10 (box), 11, 12–13, 49
time line; history, 8; sample of, 52–53
tour; purpose of, 45; self-guided, 3, 4 (box); stationed, 3 (box); virtual, 38, 39, 40; *See also* thematic tour
tour development process, 8
tour review, annual (sample), 144–146
training, guide. *See* guide training
training options; enrichment activity, 64–65; lectures and tours, 63; readings, 62; study session, 63–64
transition spot, definition of, 42

virtual tour, 38, 39, 40
visitor, xii, 3; *See also* audience
visitor survey, 9
visual focal point (example), 75–76
vocal technique; articulation, 120; expression, 120–121; phonation, 119–120; relaxation, 118; resonance, 119–120
volunteer, 12, 127, 131